Lead Soldiers and Figurines

Lead Soldiers
and
Figurines

By

MARCEL BALDET

Honorary Member of the Society of
Collectors of Historical Figurines, Paris

General Secretary of La Sabretache, Paris

With Foreword by PETER J. BLUM
President, Military Historical Society
New York N.Y.

Translated by
E. STANTON RUSSELL

CROWN PUBLISHERS, Inc. NEW YORK, N.Y.

Jacket illustration

JOUSTING KNIGHTS
Flat figurines. Height 65 mm. Arms and helmet visors are articulated.
By Besold, circa 1835.

CONTENTS

FOREWORD

The great soldiers of history and the armies they led are too often confined to dull facts in musty old volumes. Yet, as one looks at military figurines arrayed in battle order, history starts to come alive. The model soldier has an intriguing ability to telescope both time and space. Each small soldier can accurately depict the uniforms and weapons of the day. In the space of a few feet the climax of a great battle can unfold; before your very eyes cavalries charge, infantries fall and artilleries roar, at the battle of Waterloo or Yorktown, at Belleau Wood or Pork Chop Hill.

To those who collect lead soldiers and figurines, history has a special meaning. Each war, each engagement, becomes a challenge to be condensed to miniature. The professional historian and maker of figurines achieve this goal with spectacular success.

The name of Marcel Baldet is known the world over. He has written, not only for the important European publications, but for leading American magazines of military history. The journal of the Company of Military Collectors and Historians has made excellent use of Mr. Baldet's wealth of knowledge about French troops serving in America. Adjutant's Call, *the journal of the Military Historical Society, has invoked his talents to write about the French Army of Napoleon.*

Mr. Baldet's fine hand for making figurines is evidenced in many outstanding private collections and museums. He brings to figure-making great craftsmanship and a unique understanding of military history. These same qualities are profoundly evident in Lead Soldiers and Figurines.

PETER J. BLUM.

Above: TRAINING. *Eighteenth century Dutch figurine, of silver. Height, 40 mm. (Collection of Mme. J. Ruby, Paris.)* Below: ENTERING PARIS THROUGH LA PORTE ST. MARTIN KING LOUIS XV AND HIS DAUGHTERS, EN ROUTE FROM COMPIENGNE *(sic). Circa 1770. A very rare group of cardboard soldiers, by J. B. Lesueur. (Collection of Bidault de Lisle, Carnavalet Museum, Paris.)* ▶

TO THE READER

Why say "figurine" and not simply "lead soldier", as in the good old days? First of all, because there are no lead soldiers, for those that were thus described were made of tin. And then again, because the term "figurine" fortunately is applicable to all small-scale figures representing personages in constumes of various ages, civilian as well as military, and without distinction as to the materials from which they are made.

In fifty years the little "tin soldier", that most modest of all toys, has after many transformations become a collector's item. In the past twenty years throughout the world, the figurine has seen the doors of museums open before it.

That fact, I believe, is unique. But it is surprising for other reasons as well. While the average collector is content to assemble rare, costly, unique, or just unusual items for his personal satisfaction, we are here concerned with the devotee who is himself responsible for their creation, either personally or via the talents of another. The value of the resulting exhibits rests entirely in the research necessary to create them, as well as the ingenuity, skill, and art with which they are executed.

This rapid rise has occurred in our lifetime, and by illustrating examples that are both typical and comprehensive, I have tried to demonstrate it in a straightforward manner.

I have deliberately only briefly touched on its early aspects, mentioning only essential names in the desire to avoid tiresome enumerations for the reader, while still enabling him to satisfy his curiosity in acquiring some knowledge of the activities and specialities developed in different countries.

This study is therefore neither an honor roll nor a catalogue listing of all the outstanding artists in the field. It is rather an unpretentious study allowing us to judge where the figurine stands today, not only for the individual as a document on the history of costuming, but also for general educational purposes.

It is thanks to the collectors themselves that we have been able to assemble so diversified a group of illustrations. They all responded to our request with the alacrity and courtesy that are among the characteristics of the international world of the figurine.

If my objectives have been attained, it is to the collector that I owe my thanks.

MARCEL BALDET.

Above, left: HORSE GUARD. *Second Empire, circa 1854;* right: OFFICER OF THE EIGHTH HUSSARDS. *Circa 1854. Height 18 cm.* Below, left to right: FIELD MARSHAL RADETSKY, EMPEROR FRANCIS JOSEPH, COLONEL-GENERAL PEJACZEVICZ OF THE HUNGARIAN HUSSARS. *Height 13 cm. Of molded paper, painted. Arms and accessories of cast tin. (Collection of the author.)*

ANCIENT IMAGES OF MAN

Representations of animals and of human beings are as old as man himself. The discovery, in caves that are well-nigh inaccessible, of countless sketches, paintings, and crude clay statuettes dating back to prehistoric times has presented researchers with a dilemma.

That the caves were not suitable for human habitation is evident from their very arrangement. They must have served as sanctuaries, and their decorations, almost certainly esoteric, must have had some connection with rituals of witchcraft, or with the conjuration of evil spirits.

In 1902, excavations conducted by Sir Arthur Evans among the ruins of the palace of Minos, at Knossos, brought to light a remarkable series of feminine statuettes, made of alabaster or of steatite, and dating back some three thousand years. Those miniature statues forever disposed of the former theory that pre-Hellenic costume had consisted solely of draped garments.

During that same period, civilization in Egypt was more advanced than in any other part of the world. And in the tomb of Prince Emsah (Twelfth Dynasty) of several centuries later was found the extraordinary collection of soldiers, Egyptian and Negro, that is now displayed in the Cairo Museum. Those little figures, of carved and painted wood, are unquestionably the most characteristic prototypes of military figurines.

The Egyptian soldiers—tall, thin, well built, and with clean-cut profiles—are uniformly clad in linen loincloths with triangular front flaps. Infantrymen, they are armed either with short javelins and decorated ogival shields, or with long, straight swords, without handguards, that are carried as though they were large church candles. These soldiers, who could never be confused with the flat-nosed black mercenaries or with Semites, are surrounded by the countless figurines customarily found in the burial places

Much closer to our lives are the decorated terra cotta figurines discovered in Greece, at Tanagra and Delphos. They re-create for us, most realistically, a world in miniature that seems more authentic than do the masterpieces of ancient sculpture. They acquaint us with the housewife kneading dough and with the bald and somewhat seedy pedagogue; with the young schoolgirl and the strolling peddler crying his wares, with the feminine acrobatic dancer, and with a horde more.

By the infinite variety of their silhouettes,

THE TOWN CRIER. *Of polychrome terra cotta. From Tanagra. Discovered between 1872 and 1875. (Louvre Museum, Paris.)*

ERRATA

Page 37. Caption to plate. *For* 'Extra large' *read* 'Collector'.
Page 41. Caption to lower plate. *For* 'Extra large' *read* 'Collector'.

NOTE

Pages 113-114. Norman Newton Ltd, famous for their *ronde-bosse* miniatures in the 33 mm. size, employ some twenty-five artists, specialists in their work. In the early days of the firm new models were added at rare intervals, but now Norman Newton Ltd add regularly to their list and produce a sumptuous catalogue which in itself is a real documented work on models.

attitudes, and dress, those objects from many countries and of many epochs provide the archeologist with sources that are at once more valuable and more complete than sketches or paintings, and more informative than engravings on stone, bone, or wood.

Why? Because they present us, even though the scale is small, with a configuration of three dimensions—a concise definition of sculpture. Their creator, whether artist or humble modeler, whether working with clay, stone, wood, or bronze, saw, and therefore revealed to us, all sides of his model.

Regardless of their age or of the materials from which they are made, human figurines may be divided into two very distinct categories. The first is religious in character and the figurines represent gods or patron saints. In the second, perquisite of childhood, they take the form of dolls or toys.

Throughout the Middle Ages, *plombs* representing St. Michael, St. George, St. Christopher,

PRINCE EMSAH'S GUARD *(12th Dynasty). Part of group in polychrome wood. From tomb discovered at Assiout, Upper Egypt. Circa 2000 B.C. (Cairo Museum.)* ▶
▼

or the Virgin Mary, or having the symbolic shape of hearts or shells, were peddled at very low prices to the multitudes of pilgrims that thronged the roads of France, Germany, and Italy. Those objects, usually detailed on only one surface, were cast in tin or lead *(plomb)*- hence the name. And although they were produced in considerable quantities, they were so fragile that very few have come down to us. Some typical examples are on view at the Musée de Cluny, in Paris.

Toward the end of the last century, much excitement was caused by the discovery, in the bed of the Seine, of small lead soldiers which the experts of that day assigned to the reign of Henry IV. Amateur collectors of the unusual displayed great interest in those ancient curios, which appeared in increasing numbers, thanks to repeated and fruitful dredgings. Some of the increase was also due to the ingenious work of facsimile specialists, who, with clever counterfeits, exploited the unlimited credulity of the

SLAVE TAKING A YOUNG GIRL TO SCHOOL. *Of polychrome terra cotta. From Tanagra. Discovered between 1872 and 1875. (Louvre Museum, Paris.)*

purchasers. Roger Vaultier, to whom collectors are indebted for serious research on the origin of figurines, has recently resolved the question [1].

Mention may here be made of the decorated bronze figures that comprise the crew of the famous "Charles V" *nef* (medieval sailing ship), crafted by German goldsmiths of the sixteenth century and now on display at the Musée des Arts et Métiers, in Paris. Such objects, however, are somewhat beyond the scope of the present work. They are automatons, actuated by an ingenious arrangement of gears.

In the treatise cited above, Roger Vaultier (at that time associated with the Department of Medals of the National Library) writes in interesting detail of toys belonging to the future Louis XIII, for whom the Queen, Marie de Médicis, commissioned goldsmith Nicolas Roger to fashion three hundred little men of silver. In 1610, the year of the assassination of Henry IV, they were supplemented by little men of lead, which could be drawn up in battalions. Then came field pieces and, probably to augment the total number of effectives, small soldiers made of earthenware.

Louis XIV, as a child, also had an army made of silver—infantry, cavalry, and cannon—produced by Chassel the sculptor and Merlin the goldsmith, at the not inconsiderable cost of 50,000 *écus*. Those troops were inherited by the Dauphin, who then acquired lead soldiers modeled and cast in Alsace at the instance of the great Colbert. He likewise commanded a cardboard army, comprised of twenty cavalry squadrons and ten infantry battalions, and painted at a cost of 30,000 *livres* by Pierre Couturier, who was directed to execute the work "for the amusement and instruction of the Dauphin".

Unfortunately, there is not a single example extant of those little silver figures, which during the later days of misfortune, were sent to the melting pot, along with the great king's silver service.

At about that time, Parisian pewterers and makers of knickknacks began to produce toy dishes—platters, plates, and pitchers—as well as miniature reilgious articles—crosses, candlesticks, and censers. They also, of course, produced toy soldiers.

[1] Prestige des Figurines Historiques, 1956.

THE BIRTH OF THE TIN SOLDIER

Toward the close of the seventeenth century there began to appear, on both sides of the Rhine, the first manufacturers worthy of the name. At Strasbourg, the Bergmann workshop turned out the protagonists of the Seven Years War—the troops of Louis XV and Frederick II. At Nuremberg, Hilpert Brothers offered a variety of subjects—farm people, wild and domestic animals, soldiers, and one need scarcely add, Old Fritz and his guard, as well as contemporary personalities of importance.

At the beginning, these characters, of varying heights, were cast in pure tin. That metal, fragile, flexible, and high in price, soon gave way to a stronger alloy of tin and lead. But they continued to be known as "tin soldiers", or *Zinnfigur,* as they are still called today.

Success gave rise to imitation. New foundries appeared—at Berlin, where Catel was established and, significantly, at Erfurt. For a while Erfurt became a center of production in which engraving was mediocre and coloring so poor that it could scarcely be called painting.

During the Napoleonic Wars, production was slowed almost to a standstill until the vanquished Emperor became a legend. Then his Grand Army and his allies—Bavaria, Baden, Hesse, Saxony, Wurtemberg, Holland, Switzerland, and Italy—

provided the central theme for contemporary novelties as did Napoleon's adversaries, the English, Russians and Austrians.

Nuremberg quickly took the lead in German production, which had thus far known no serious competition. In Nuremberg were Ammon and Son, Schweigger, Gottschalk, Haffner, and the Heinrichssens, who in father-and-son succession operated from 1839 until just before the outbreak of World War II, encountering no worthy competition save that of Allgeyer, at Erfurt.

Came now, about 1840, the heyday of the so-called "flat" figurines, which, it should be recognized, enjoy the benefit of an unusual combination of circumstances. There was the great growth of railroads throughout Europe, appropriately commemorated by the charming "Nuremberg Railroad at Furth", which is illustrated in color on page 45.

The spreading rail network revolutionized commercial relations throughout the continent and facilitated the exportation of new toys, which became increasingly attractive, reflecting

RENAISSANCE CANNONEER. *Flat figurine, engraved on one side only. Not painted. Early nineteenth century. By* HEINRICHSSEN. *(Focke Collection, Leverkusen.)*

as they did a time that was rife with exciting events. Acceptance of the new toys was in nowise hindered by the low prices at which they were offered.

Europe rediscovered Antiquity, as excavations and findings in Egypt were followed by those in Greece and Italy. In literature and in art, this was the full flush of the romantic period. The vogue was for the troubadour style, for medieval reconstructions that were often of doubtful authenticity. There was a proliferation of knights in helmets and plumes and of ladies in tall, tapering headdresses—and even, an anachronism of several centuries, of musketeers.

As the nineteenth century progressed, France conquered Algeria and preparations were made for expeditions to the heart of black Africa.

ROYAL SPANISH GUARD, *1830. Lancer. One of the first tin soldiers made in Spain. By Portolli. (Almirall Fusté Collection, Barcelona.)*

Above, left: KNIGHTS IN TOURNAMENT. *Flat figurines 7 cm. high. Engraved, on one side only, by F. Engels. Painting by Onken. Circa 1840;* above right: THE MADONNA OF ANDECHS. *Flat figurine. Engraved by Schweizer. Height, 11 cm.* Below, left: THE HOLY FAMILY; below right: THE THREE WISE MEN. *Flat figurines. Engraved by Schweizer, painted by Onken. Every Christmas these groups are displayed in one of the Hamburg churches. (Onken Collection, Hamburg.)*

The Russo-Turkish War ended, after the victory of Navarin, in independence for Greece; meanwhile, England was waging war in China.

In France, a revolution followed by a coup d'état brought back the Napoleonic eagles. Intervention in Italy preceded the finding of common cause with Turkey and Great Britain for the Crimean Expedition, and for participation in the struggle in China. Soon to follow was the Mexican Campaign, and the attack on Denmark by Prussia and Austria. In the United States, the tragic War Between the States had

started. On the eve of the Franco-German conflict, there was mounting tension between Prussia and France.

For the figurine manufacturers, who were astute business men, the available subjects now offered an embarrassment of choice!

Both Heinrichssen and Allgeyer were accomplished craftsmen. They personally inspected and retouched each of their new molds, whose quality was definitely superior to that of their predecessors. Heinrichssen, although a good designer himself, commissioned well-known artists to create his new series. Thus it is that Wanderer was credited with "The Siege of Troy" and Paul Ritter with "Wallenstein's Camp", while "Gustave Adolphe at Lützen" is the work of Camphausen.

For the first steps toward standardization, credit must also be given to Heinrichssen, who decided that henceforth his foot soldiers were to have a height of 30 mm; his horsemen a height of 40 mm. Those dimensions became known as "the Nuremberg size".

Czar Nicholas I directed Heinrichssen to make reproductions of all his cavalry guard regiments. For them Heinrichssen adopted "the Berlin size", which was several millimeters taller than that of Nuremberg.

Connoisseurs have no need to look on the bases of his figurines for his initials *E. H.* Heinrichssen is instantly identified by the slim, slender silhouette of his infantrymen; by the proud bearing and cleanness of leg of his horses.

Before setting up shop for himself, Allgeyer had worked for Heinrichssen as an engraver, and his son was to belong to the same school. We are especially indebted to him for his troubadour series, and for tournament participants of enchanting romanticism. Until his death, toward the end of the nineteenth century, he was the principal source of supply for the French market.

It is clearly impossible to give a resumé of the output of these two founders, whose work may be said to encompass universal history, from the siege of Troy down to the most recent colonial expeditions. Obviously much attention was concentrated on campaigns of the Revolution and of the Empire, as well as on the military forces of Germany.

MILITARY CHESSMEN. *End of First Empire. Flat figurines of unknown origin. Heights, 6.5 to 8 cm. (Sabretache Collection, Paris.)*

LANSQUENET FIFE AND DRUM. *Second half of sixteenth century. Engraved on one side. First appearance early nineteenth century. (Focke Collection, Leverkusen.)*

Tribute having been paid to the two foremost founders, mention should also be made of Denecke and of Wegmann at Brunswick; of Haffner at Erfurt; of Haselbach at Berlin; and of the Rieche Brothers and Du Bois at Hanover. Their figurines, it must be admitted, were inferior, in choice of subjects and in quality, to those of their predecessors.

All founders, at that time, wholesaled their painted figurines by weight—actually by the pound. The packages were oval boxes of thin wood, whose covers were decorated with reproductions of medals awarded at various expositions. These boxes had a net content of 2 ounces, 4 ounces, 8 ounces, and one pound. Of them, the two largest contained from 75 to 150 assorted pieces, including infantry, cavalry and artillery, together with such accessories as trees, siege baskets, houses, and groves of small trees.

Other collections consisted of wagons, tents, cannon, and caissons. Boxes having a weight of 4 ounces and 2 ounces generally represented only one arm of the service: infantry, cavalry, artillery, or the engineer corps. Every box was accompanied by a printed announcement, which was often supplemented by a map suggesting battle order. Thus for the benefit of German children, there was patriotic propaganda with pedagogic intent.

By 1900, the Heinrichssen catalog commanded a wholesale price of 3.90 francs. A box containing two ounces of soldiers was retailed at prices ranging from 0.85 to 1.00 francs. Even at that time, such prices could be explained only by extremely low wage rates. The women who did the painting, at home, earned no more than five or six marks a week; they are scarcely to be blamed for the inconsistent and inaccurate coloring which today shocks the veriest neophyte.

In Paris, the "Nuremberg boxes" could be had either at the "Plat d'Etain", on the rue des Saints-Pères, or from Coisel's on the rue Dunquerque, billed as "the exclusive representative and distributor of Heinrichssen". Thither, on Thursdays [1], flocked an ever-increasing crowd of school boys, attracted by the very low prices.

But, of an evening, Coisel's small shop was invaded by gentlemen of some importance who engaged in polite but heated discussions surprising in such a place. After purchasing the "large" boxes in quantity, they proceeded seriously to reconstruct famous battles, mobilizing for that purpose thousands of infantry and cavalry. Some of them mounted, on large sheets of cardboard, collections representing warriors of all kinds, in varying battle dress. Classified by countries and constantly enriched by additions, these tableaux made a remarkable documentation that eliminated much research on the part of the collector.

About them we shall presently have an opportunity to learn much more.

[1] Throughout France, schools are closed on Thursdays.

SENOT, DRUM MAJOR OF THE CONSULAR GUARD *(He later became drum major of the Imperial Grenadier Guard). Height 70 mm., not including headgear. Engraving is exceptionally fine. One copy, also unpainted, may be seen at the Army Museum, in Paris. (Collection of the author.)*

THE FIRST LEAD SOLDIERS

Did true, in-the-round lead soldiers—those sculptured in three dimensions, with shapes determined solely by the molds in which they were cast—first see the light of day in Nuremberg or in Paris? That question has long been argued, but never settled.

Certain it is that in Paris, shortly after the revolution of 1789, Lucotte made soldiers of that kind. In 1828 three other Parisian craftsmen, Cuberly, Blondel, and Gerbeau, joined forces to produce, under the trade mark *C.B.G.*, solid infantrymen and cavalrymen.

The manufacture of in-the-round figurines was clearly more complicated than the production of flat ones, which were complete as they came from the molds. For instance, a rider was cast separately from the horse he was to be astride. Here, however, there was an incidental advantage: the same steed could be employed for horsemen of various kinds. Some manufacturers abused that opportunity by disregarding the difference in trappings between the horses of hussars, dragoons and cuirassiers!

The pure lead originally employed was found

MUSICIANS OF THE IMPERIAL GUARD. *First Hussars, carabineer with trumpeter, voltigeur, and sapper of the Guard Engineers. Ronde-bosse figurines by Lucotte. (Philippot Collection, Paris.)*

to be subject to the limitations encountered with tin. Especially with respect to the mass of metal necessary for casting horses, lead was too soft; legs tended to become deformed under the weight of the body. Much time was to pass, however, before that metal was replaced by an alloy of lead (15 per cent) and antimony, (25 per cent) exactly like that now employed in the casting of printer's type. The addition of antimony to lead causes the alloy to expand as the molten metal solidifies, and thus to fill the tiniest incisions of the mold.

The new alloy was first used for soldiers from the Revolution and especially from the wars of the First Empire. The literature of that day was fostering the "Napoleonic legend", which climaxed in the return and burial of the Emperor's remains at the Invalides.

The new toys, although much more expensive than those hitherto known, immediately enjoyed great success in France. They were larger than the tin soldiers, less fragile, and easier to maneuver. The arms were jointed at the shoulders and could take various positions. The heads, attached to a sort of stem, could be turned from left to right. Horses had movable legs, and saddles and shabracks were sometimes removable.

Finally, the packaging of soldiers and accessories, in cartons bearing pictures, proved most attractive to the children for whom they were intended.

When confronted by such improvements, the manufacturers of Nuremberg and of Hanover did not rest on their laurels. After experimenting with new models, which were called "solids" as opposed to the "flats", they brought out a compromise: a "half-in-the-round" product, made in a two-piece mold like that employed for tin soldiers, but so deeply sculptured as to exhibit high relief. True three-dimensional form, however, was not achieved.

The result, excellent for small and acceptable for medium sizes, was much less satisfactory for figurines having a height of 8 cm. The engraver was faced with difficult technical problems, given the large mass of metal involved and the fact that, as it came from the mold, the subject was complete in every detail. In consequence, the larger silhouette figurines, of which only the profile was fashioned with care, had a bizarre appearance when viewed head on.

Allgeyer and Haffner, who specialized in that type of production for export (the German market remained ever faithful to the *Zinnfiguren*), enjoyed marked commercial success. Their "half-in-the-round" figurines were lighter, and hence subject to lower import duties. Their prices, far below those of the solid models, made it easy to meet competition.

During the Second Empire, the Mignot establishment in Paris absorbed two older French firms, Lucotte and C.B.G. The trade marks of both, as found in the molds obtained from them, were continued.

Mignot developed collections covering all the great periods of history, as well as models of the armies of Italy, Germany, Austria, Russia, and England; and he produced such exotic series as East Indians, redskins, Chinese, and Africans. The same firm initiated an excellent

FRENCH INFANTRY STANDARD-BEARERS. *1728. Galley flag at center. Painting by Jullemier and Bürkhalter. (Philippot Collection, Paris.)*

collection of important historical personages, to which frequent additions were made. Until the eve of the First World War, Mignot was the unquestioned leader in the production of true, in-the-round lead soldiers.

75 MM. FIELD PICE. *Ronde-Bosse figurines by Lucotte. (Philippot Collection, Paris.)*

A NEW SCIENCE:
THE MILITARY UNIFORM

The renaissance of France, less than twenty years after her defeat by Germany in 1871, was marked by the Universal Exposition held in Paris in 1889. In the Army Pavilion were gathered together priceless historical relics, which, together with associated paintings and sculpture, comprised a veritable museum of military glory.

The moment was well chosen. The country had courageously returned to work. The army, re-formed and reorganized, had regained the admiration of the people. It had been furnished with new standards to replace the "temporary flags" of wool bunting, which lacked both inscriptions and gold lace.

The daily press of that period reflects both the military revival and the enthusiasm of the people, to whom the plenitude of emotion-provoking exhibits seemed the symbol of a magnificent and heroic past.

At the close of the Exposition, a group of artists, historians and scholars associated themselves with two painters of wartime scenes, Meissonier and Edouard Detaille, to form a society known as "La Sabretache". Their primary objective was to establish a permanent military museum, and to further that objective, they produced a monthly publication, *Le Carnet,* which included studies on arms, uniforms, military headdress, and kindred topics.

Membership grew rapidly. Success was achieved when, in 1896, an official decree auth-orized the museum. Thanks to the energy of its first director, the scholarly General Vanson, it was opened in 1897, in the historic setting of the Hôtel des Invalides.

From many sources came contributions; some of them were in cash, but the more important were historical materials and souvenirs that are dazzling to present-day viewers.

The movement generated an increasing number of studies and publications concerned with the army, its uniforms, and its equipment, and from then on, there was a growing interest on the part of the public, which became enthralled with the new subject. Certainly, the science of the military uniform was not new, but it had hitherto been the perquisite of painters and engravers who specialized in military subjects and needed documentation for illustrations commissioned by publishers—and of a few widely scattered and almost unknown lovers of military accoutrements. In the preceding pages we have glimpsed the elementary, unconnected, and disparate origins of an interest that later produced a hitherto unknown personage: the collector of military figurines.

Above, left: OFFICERS AND ARTILLERYMEN OF THE IMPERIAL FOOT GUARD; above, right: BELGIAN LANCER OF THE FIRST REGIMENT, 1900. Below, left: FRENCH LIGHT HORSE - CRACK COMPANY OF THE SIXTH REGIMENT, 1812; below, right: FOUR-CALIBER FIELDPIECE. *Gribeauval design. Ronde-bosse figur. (Almirall Fusté Collection, Barcelona.)* ▶

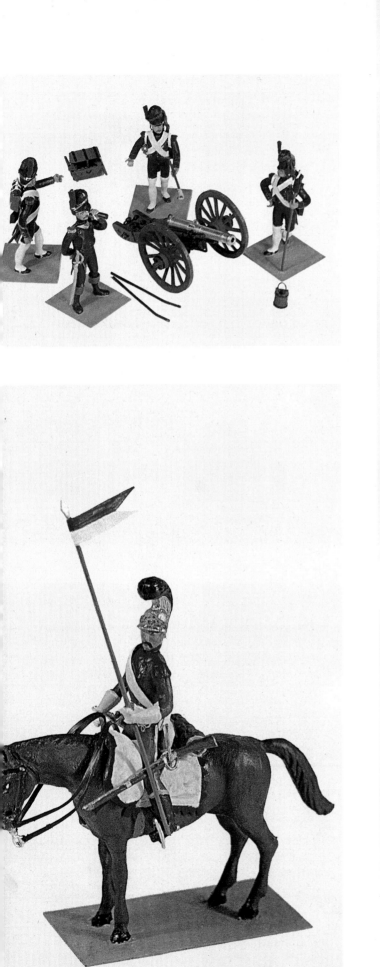

THE COLLECTOR

Curiosity is not a taste for the good, or for the beautiful, but for the thing that is rare; for something one possesses that others do not have. It is not a pastime; it is a passion. It is not a passion for the unusual thing of momentary vogue, but rather for a definite rarity that has earned popularity.

LA BRUYERE *De La Mode*

It is doubtful whether that definition of the lover of curiosities in the days of the Great Century is strictly applicable to the collector of figurines as he is known today. He lacks it would seem, the characteristics of "the well-brought-up man in the grip of the secret vice", as described by Balzac in *Le Cousin Pons*.

What, then, is a collector?

His origin, in France, goes back to about 1900, and to the small shop of the senior Coisel, where there assembled a group of gentlemen with a common interest in the boxes of tin soldiers then offered for sale. Among them were MM. Ridder, Ternisien, and Lecomte, Colonel Mossman, and Count MacGregor, a

◄ Above: ZOUAVE *and* GRENADIER OF THE IMPERIAL GUARD. Below: CUIRASSIER *and* CARABINEER. *Height of horsemen, exclusive of base, 35 cm. Trial castings in bronze of figurines executed by the sculptor Frémiet for Napoleon III. Originals, of painted plaster, were destroyed during Tuileries fire in 1871. (Brunon Collection, Marseilles.)*

former artillery officer of Her Gracious Majesty Queen Victoria. There were physicians, as well, including Dr. Héry, and most important of all, Dr. Laumonnier to whom we owe the priceless heritage of the initial color reproductions that occupied eight pages in the Christmas edition of *L'Illustration* for 1899/1900. From that work we have borrowed many examples that, with the passage of time, have become precious historical documents.

Without working together, and probably without acquaintance, people in different places originated the idea of using toy soldiers, which then were the common property of children everywhere, to develop a pastime that was known, simply, as "The Game of the Lead Soldiers".

Some found it interesting to recreate great battles of the Empire, for which they found, in the famous Nuremberg boxes, the necessary infantry, cavalry, artillery, corps of engineers, and headquarters staff. The boxes also provided as accessories elements of terrain, as well as battle maps. It was a short step forward to organize operations more serious than had been contemplated for children. The enthusiasts had only to consult the books in their libraries—

GRENADIER COMPANY OF THE THIRD SWISS REGIMENT. *Period of Louis XVI. (By, and from the Collection of, C.F. Keller, Paris.)*

THE OLYMPIC GAMES *(500 B.C.). Flat figurines. By Kiel. (Wattier Collection, Paris.)*

rooms that, naturally, then became battle-grounds.

Such an entreprise, as Dr. Laumonnier recounts, required not only large numbers of effectives, but also much space and time. As one example, he cites his own reconstruction of the final phase of the Battle of Austerlitz, when the enemy columns, pinched between the divisions of Davout and of Soult, were driven back onto the frozen lake at Satschau. Consideration being given to the scale (1 to 50 or 1 to 100) adopted for the combatants and the terrain alike, he made use of "only" four thousand pieces, on a field of battle "scarcely" twelve yards square.

When one considers the time consumed in preparing essential features of that battleground, and when one realizes that it is impossible to place in position more than 400 or 500 pieces in an hour, it becomes evident that the doctor was occupied for several successive evenings, during which, obviously, the room chosen for the combat was out of bounds for all other members of the family. Came then the duty

of disassembling the display, and of arranging its components in labeled boxes in readiness for the next battle!

Less energetic buffs—the platonic lovers of the game—were content to amass troop concentrations. In formations not widely dispersed, they assembled battalions, squads of cavalry, and batteries of artillery, which were passed in review. A regiment of infantry at battle strength, when drawn up in columns of four on a terrain in scale with the pieces, actually occupied twenty-five yards. The same men, marshalled as battalions in line, required a depth of only 24 to 32 inches, but the front then had a width of four yards.

A third category, the "warriors," quickly exhausted the possibilities of that kind of play. They progressed to military exercises that were infinitely more complex, and more productive of unexpected happenings. No longer was it a question of reconstructing an engagement. No longer was the enemy represented by proxy. He was present. The object was to give battle, in accordance with an original plan, with effectives and reserves allocated; with the zones of combat delineated; with the weather conditions prescribed. Conventional rules were rigidly applied, in the presence of an umpire whose decisions, as at formal military maneuvers, was final, and not subject to appeal.

This was a veritable *kriegspiel,* with troop movements on quadrilled maps, with reconnaissance and deployment up to the moment of contact on a large-scale map of a terrain mutually defined at the outset. Everything was planned and timed to the minute, including liaisons, the crossing of streams and rivers, and the advance of supply and munition trains, which, of course, could be delayed or destroyed by the fire of distant enemy artillery.

A few years ago, one of the few living witnesses of those bygone days recounted that Colonel MacGregor (who has already been mentioned, and who, besides being a noted Egyptologist, was a brother-in-law of the philosopher Bergson) had formulated *kriegspiel* rules so precise and so comprehensive that they are still followed by adherents who engage in the noble game today.

Writing of that game inevitably brings to mind those chapters of the novel *Axelle,* in which Pierre Benoit so vividly and graphically describes that extraordinary *kriegspiel* session between Baron de Reichendorf, a retired Prussian general, and Dumaine, the French sergeant who was a prisoner of war.

Here, to be sure, the novelist intervenes to explain that "... when two opposing units came face to face in the same square, the General, who was philosophically versed in military matters, invoked the goddess of chance, and the decision was based on the fall of dice!" Truly a magnificent concept. The same procedure may perhaps have been followed during the second half of the nineteenth century when young officers in training at the General Staff School were called upon to resolve difficult problems on the map or in the sandbox.

Is all this a far cry from collectors and collections?

Some enthusiasts, as we have said, set up representative tableaux that were in effect explanatory catalogs of the troops they possessed. Their experience closely paralleled the adventures of a woman who lives on the other side of the Atlantic, and who shall be nameless, despite the fact that she will be quickly identified by some readers!

HUNTING SCENES IN THE DAYS OF LOUIS XV. *After original sketches by Rousselot. Engraved by S. Maier. (By, and from the collection of C.F. Keller, Paris.)*

When she was married, some thirty years ago, she and her husband embarked upon the classic grand tour of Europe. Before returning, they had traveled through France, Germany, Austria, Switzerland, and Italy. Their baggage then included curios and souvenirs from many countries. Not the least important were lead soldiers, acquired hither and yon, which my friend proceeded to display in showcases and on the shelves in her library. She and her friends were entranced by the decorative effect. The bright colors of the little soldiers contrasted most pleasantly with the leather bindings.

"One evening," she recounts (and I have the story directly from the heroine herself), "I was struck by a horrid thought. What if the uniforms of this grenadier, and of this hussar, are not truly authentic? What if the painter made a mistake?"

On the morrow, she made a serious but unsuccessful effort at verification. Neither in books that she owned, nor in those that she borrowed from a nearby library, could she find precise information.

But, as a woman of parts and of a methodical turn of mind, she was not to be easily rebuffed. She made inquiries at her bookstore and at other booksellers, which were relayed by them to their European correspondents. As books

See caption p. 21.

and albums written in German, English, and French began to arrive, she was, for the moment, overjoyed. There were catalogs too, from every country in Europe. Little by little, the influx of volumes forced the retreat of the little soldiers, who were driven from bookcases to closets, and from closets to boxes that were stowed away wherever space could be found. After bookshelves had been installed in other rooms, a secretary was engaged to index and catalog the works that continued to pour in. The secretary became a librarian, who today has charge of what is probably the finest and most complete military library in the world.

Whenever an important public sale is announced in London, Paris, Brussels, or Hamburg, orders are dispatched to an agent to acquire, perhaps, a collection of prints that may have been sought in vain over a period of many years. If the item is of capital importance, the lady, who does not leave major decisions to others, promptly boards the next plane.

It is not to be thought, however, that she risks the pitfall inherent in the words of La Bruyère at the beginning of this chapter! All of her purchases are critically studied, and carefully compared with known works on the same subject. So thorough is her background of research that I have heard this "expert" in the science of the military uniform completely confound the curator of the Army Museum

when she questioned the date of a military exhibit.

Obviously, and for good reason, experiences of that order were not enjoyed by collectors during the Heroic Period, that is to say during the very first years of this century. But, after close and continued study of their "tableaux," they became aware of shortcomings. They realized that the painting was decidedly mediocre; that there were flagrant, if inevitable, errors requiring correction. They could not, in fact, condone inaccuracies that meant very little to those of their friends whose interest was limited to troops, as such, and to tactics.

Paul Armont, the dramatist, together with his collaborator and inseparable friend, Léopold Marchand, decided that the time had come to apply paint remover to the military figurines and have them repainted, accurately, in harmony with dependable documents they possessed. After some search, they located a painter, Hamel by name, who over a period of many years meticulously refinished toy soldiers that, after leaving his hands, became the showpieces of important collections. Armont and Marchand then planned to round out some series that were considered incomplete, and to arrange for their production in France.

That project, unhappily, was brought to an end by World War I, during which some of the associated pioneers were to become witnesses, participants, and victims.

See caption p. 21.

BETWEEN TWO WARS

Immediately after World War I, there was an apparent lessening of interest in military affairs, a not unnatural consequence of four years of unremitting combat. No historical publications issued during the opening years of the century would appear to have survived. There were no new books, aside from those directly concerned with that war, to whet the appetite of the handful of remaining collectors, who, however, did not remain inactive.

Paul Armont assembled a small group with whom he proceeded to reinvigorate his temporarily abandoned project. For him, Victor Hamel, Bombled, and Lucien Rousselot designed the first models of a brilliant series, to which new subjects were added in due course.

Mignot, who was to produce the new collections, looked in vain for engravers in France. He therefore called upon foreign specialists: Maier, at Erfurt, Frank, and Hahnemann. Among painters already skilled in an extremely delicate technique, he enlisted L. Rousselot, Cosson, Madame Métayer, Mademoiselle Sainte-Marie, and, of course, the accomplished Hamel. Those artists, benefitting from increasingly meticulous research, applied their talents to the perfection of figurine subjects that had nothing whatever in common with those of the relatively recent past.

Very properly, credit was given to the designer, the engraver, and the painter, whose names were printed in connection with those of the group that had planned and produced the work. Bold innovators achieved transformations that hitherto had not been considered possible. The head of one figurine was soldered to the body of another. By a similar procedure, attitudes were varied by changing the position of arms and legs.

No finer figurines are known than those that adorn the pages of the Mignot catalog: Aztecs, Assyrians, Egyptians, the House of Valois, the Knights of the Golden Fleece, and the trophies of the Battle of Austerlitz which, in the years that followed, were supplemented by other marvelous creations.

Paul Armont and his old friend Léopold Marchand were now joined by recent recruits to the ranks of figurine enthusiasts: Roger de Dampierre, Pierre de Lanux, Valery Larbaud, Pierre Simon, Fernand Gravey, Maurice Lairez, and two scholarly citizens of Strasbourg, Paul Martin and M. Brétégnier. Furthermore, that tireless, animating spirit Armont engaged in running correspondence with artists, collectors and manufacturers in other lands. Many of them—each a specialist in a particular period—entered into collaboration. Wilké, of Vienna, shared his knowledge of the Thirty Years War. Otto Gottstein, of Leipzig, spoke with authority on the days of earliest antiquity. R. G. Osterreicher concentrated on the time of the Blue King—the Great Elector of Bavaria, Max Emmanuel, known also as the destroyer of the Turks. Co-operation was also given by Biebel and Müller of Berlin, Madariaga of Madrid, and many others.

In Paris, C.-F. Keller turned out the famous "Hunts of Louis XV," of which we illustrate several pieces painted by W. Douchkine and Burkhalter (p.21-23). The molds were cut by S. Maier, after drawings by L. Rousselot. Keller also produced infantry of the days of Louis XV and Louis XVI, Swiss Guards of the same period, the Guard Cavalry of 1858, and the Second Empire Guards. Finally, in collaboration with Jean Brutsch, he developed the 1805-1815 series of infantry, full face.

In the world of the figurine, a minor revolution was occasioned by the appearance of the collector-manufacturer who, at his own expense, created models not intended for sale. The resulting *de luxe* soldier was made available only to friends who were also collectors.

Once again honor came to the little tin soldier. In the Christmas, 1928, edition of *L'Illustration* appeared an article admirably illustrated in color, on the Armont Collection. This was an

Above: EGYPTIAN DANCERS. Below: GREEK WARRIORS IN COUNCIL. *Flat figurines, painted by A. Mathiot. (Mathiot Collection, Chantilly.)* ▶

24

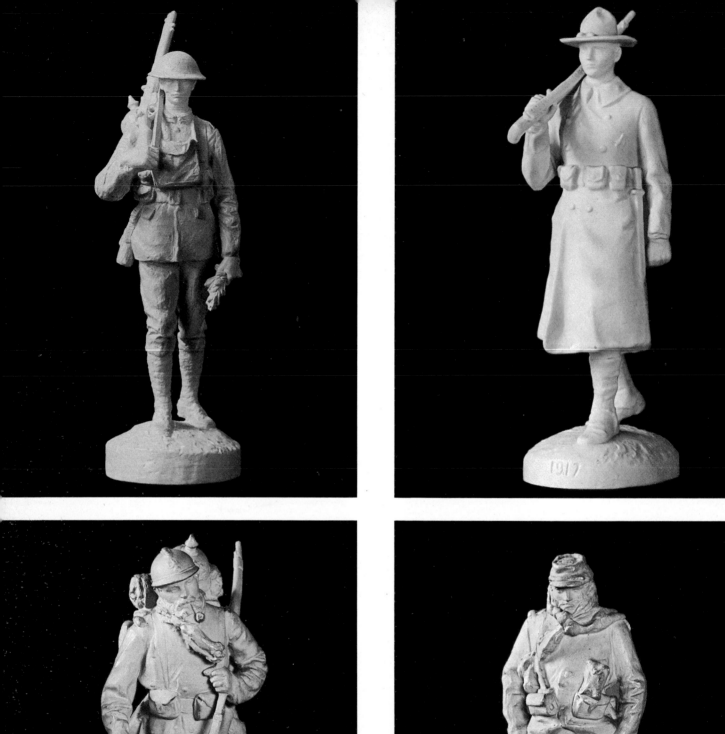

accolade, bearing witness to the progress made, in less than twenty-eight years, by the little soldiers of Nuremberg!

In the spring of 1929, in the rue de Châteaudun shop of a dealer in antiques, Armont and Marchand presented the first public exhibition in Paris ever devoted to lead soldiers as an art.

Armont displayed, on board mounts, his entire collection, ranging from Assyrians to combatants of World War I. Marchand presented historical events exactly reproduced with the aid of tin figurines. (Such exhibits were not yet known as dioramas.) There were twenty-three showcases, whose contents represented the course of history from Roman days—through the Conquest of Mexico and the Thirty Years War—to the wars of the First Empire. On November 29, 1930, a group of some fifteen collectors formed the Society of Collectors of Tin Soldiers, and elected Paul Armont president.

Germany, likewise, resumed production, with a schedule of ten thousand different figurines, covering all the armed services of all countries engaged in World War I. In 1925, a new founder, Aloys Ochel, and his accomplished engraver, Sambeth, appeared in Kiel. They rapidly moved to a dominant position in the international market. At Stuttgart, F.-C. Neckel, who relied on Frank for most of his molds, also enjoyed remarkable success. He offered a broad and varied range of subjects, from early antiquity (to which all producers on the far side of the Rhine paid great attention), to and including World War I. He likewise specialized in colonial troops, and in the American Revolution and Civil War.

Neckel, like Scholtz, frequently resorted to multiple figures: foot soldiers with three or four arms and legs differently disposed, and horses with six or seven legs. Thus, by elimination, he was able to achieve a gamut of attitudes from a minimum number of molds.

In Germany as in France, there then appeared collector-manufacturers, headed by Hahnemann at Kiel, Biebel at Berlin, and Müller at Erfurt. Most important, perhaps, was Otto Gottstein, who has already been mentioned. Many of these, after having satisfied their personal requirements, were moved to undertake production for sale, for the dual purpose of amortizing the very high costs of special production and of financing their ambitious programs for further development.

In 1930, a large number of German collectors, members of the "Klio" club, organized an International Exposition of Figurines at Leipzig. This was the beginning of the diorama, which made use of pieces produced by commercial sources and by private collectors.

During the same period, manufacturers of the in-the-round lead soldiers continued their endeavors. To their customers they made timely offerings of the leaders of World War I, as well as collections of the allies and adversaries of various nations. Mignot in Paris and W. Britain in London took the lead in troops and in *matériel*, including wagons, artillery, and tanks.

French production, although definitely superior in quality, was largely overlooked by the world of collectors, because in other countries, and particularly in the United States, emphasis was placed on complete boxes of figurines, which, on the other side of the Atlantic, represented the starting point for the majority of collectors.

It was not until 1933 that recognition was given in France to a separate category: those who collect soldiers of solid lead, and those who collect cardboard soldiers. For the variety last mentioned, as we shall see, indisputable priority rights could be advanced.

It must be admitted that, for a period of some fifteen to twenty years, those who specialized in flat soldiers exhibited toward the newcomers (whom they privately called *plombiers*[1]) the same cool if courteous condescension) formerly shown by artillery officers to their counterparts in the infantry.

This brief backward glance, which has served to recall the blooming rather than the budding of the figurine, would not be complete if we disregarded an attitude then rife with respect to the little soldiers, which were regarded as

Above, left: ENGLISH SOLDIER, *1918;* Above, right: AMERICAN SOLDIER, 1917. Below, left: POILU RETURNING FROM THE TRENCHES; Below right: POILU IN CANTONMENT. *Height, 23 cm. Of "biscuit" porcelain. by P. Ducuing.* ◄ *(Museum of the National Porcelain Factory, Sèvres.)*

[1] A play upon the word *plombier:* plumber; also one who is concerned with things made of lead.

representing a very real threat of renascent militarism.

In his preface to *L'éloge des Soldats fins* (1928), C.-F. Keller very appropriately reminds us of the municipal councillor in the Paris Hôtel de Ville who demanded that there be removed from all collections of toys destined for school children such objects as rifles, cannon, suits of armor, and lead soldiers, so that the thinking of those young people might be purged of the last germs of militarism and inoculated, instead, with the pure spirit of Locarno...

The English, recognizing that pacifism is not an attribute of childhood, concluded that the popularity of lead soldiers with the younger generation was a consequence of nationalistic policies.

If the Socialists had been victorious at the most recent elections in England, a law might have been passed prescribing that all lead soldiers be melted down before Christmas, thus terminating for all time the risk of militaristic provocation.

Was there an alternative? The *Morning Post* saw only one: prohibit the representation of wounded men or of wounded animals, as offered by the German producers; prohibit the reproduction of battle dress; and permit only the sale of soldiers in parade uniforms!

DOCUMENTATION

In the short space of four decades, the metamorphosis of the little Nuremberg soldier—from toy to figurine of tin or lead to collector's item—could not have been achieved without a corresponding development in the science of the uniform, concerning which something has already been said.

At the outset, this development was based on superficial data, often of doubtful value. Many of the earlier writers on the subject gave credence to previous writings, without bothering to check original sources.

When figurine makers like Armont, Blum of Zurich, and Ochel of Kiel undertook work on prehistoric times, Greek or Roman antiquity, the Middle Ages or the Renaissance, the only documentation to which their artists had access was often fragmentary and inadequate. Armont and the horde of French and foreign specialists who followed in his footsteps, were faced with identical problems when, indeed, they were not frustrated by a total lack of dependable documents. The iconography of those days proved at times to be of questionable worth, either because the artist had carelessly interpreted various details of accoutrement and armament or because he had given rein to his imagination. Official regulations did not always serve to clarify points of obscurity. The older the regulations, the more terse were the descriptions of uniforms. They sometimes cited only a distinctive color, or identified the metal from which a button was made. Others, however, included a precision of detail that gave to the student all the information he could ask. Example: the famous Regulation of 1812, known from the name of its compiler as "the Bardin". Its sole shortcoming is that it was not put into effect at the time it was promulgated and approved!

Lucien Rousselot could never have designed the French infantry of 1720 and 1757 if he had not conscientiously withdrawn from the War Library the Delaistre Albums, because those original source books had never been published. The creation of museums, and the establishment of large private collections in which authenticated uniforms were methodically classified, made it possible for artists and collectors critically to study headdresses, clothing, accessory equipment, horse trappings and their brass ornamentation, small arms, and decorations. Thus were corrected a multitude of errors which, firmly established, had long been accepted as truth.

In this connection, one can scarcely refrain from mentioning the most striking accomplishment of the present half-century: the collections assembled by Raoul and Jean Brunon, of Marseilles. In 1908 the two brothers, who as children had collected tin soldiers, formed the project of gathering together military souvenirs of the two previous centuries. Raoul died on the field of honor in 1917, leaving Jean, at the close of the war, to proceed single-handedly with the enterprise, to which he devoted a lifetime. Tirelessly he sought, and found, in France and in other countries, the headdresses, helmets, shields, armament and trappings used by each arm of the service in each of the periods under study. No compromise was accepted. Years, for example, were devoted to the search for the helmet worn by the dragoons under Louis XV, the finding of which was indispensable for the completion of an exhibit started twenty years earlier.

It is obviously impossible to give even a brief description of this museum, too modestly styled a collection, with its 20,000 pieces, or to enumerate the priceless relics associated with it. This sanctuary of military glory is supplemented by a highly specialized library of 25,000 volumes,

by archives, and by collections of pictures that have enabled the scholarly Brunon to resolve many a disputed question concerned with the history of uniforms or of armament. These amazing resources have enabled him to publish papers, universally accepted as authoritative, and proving of inestimable value to those collectors, in many lands, who are eager to increase their information, and their libraries.

In compiling this work, we have not hesitated to invoke the generous assistance of Jean Brunon, through whose courtesy we here present some remarkable figurines that are unusual and, at the same time, unknown to the general public.

As the fraternity of collectors increased, the tendency was toward specialization, some collectors concentrating on a particular country, some on a single epoch. They understandably had the urge to possess authentic examples (one of the pleasures of collecting) and they

progressed beyond the figurine as an end in itself to the quest of dependable documentation that is the primary concern of the specialist.

Many regimental records, often expertly illustrated, now came from the presses. In 1900, the Ministry of War issued an outstanding and most valuable compendium, *A History of French Army Corps,* which proved to be a veritable gold mine for researchers concerned with early military formations. Despite minor errors of detail, easily corrected by the specialist, it is a fundamental source book.

In Germany, Richard Knötel is publishing volume after volume of his *Uniformenkunde,* which, when completed, will comprise some two thousand annotated engravings, covering all the armies of the world.

Two compendia of illustrations, with bibliographies, should be cited: the first by Glaser (1900); the second, by Colonel Sauzey, appearing in three volumes (1901 to 1903). Although now outdated, they provide the researcher with most helpful clues.

In 1904 Malibran prepared a Collector's Guide that is a lucid and systematic abstract of uniform regulations issued for the French Army from 1780 to 1848. This eminently practical and almost error-free volume of several thousand pages, with informative tabulations, is now difficult to obtain. It is unfortunate that some devoted student has not extended its subject matter to encompass the close of the nineteenth century.

It is scarcely practical here to enumerate even the most important of the source books and picture collections that now constitute the objective of endless, and often unfruitful, investigations by figurine collectors. The several titles cited above have been named only as typical examples which may suggest the infinite effort that may be expended in quest of documentation. Mention must, however, be made of the delightful albums prepared by Job. Even today his work is a prime source of inspiration for collectors who find satisfaction in the bearing and the swagger of their little soldiers. Despite its apparent caprice (which actually constitutes the charm of his work), everything that Job has left us is authentic to the last detail.

No consideration of documentation would be complete without mention of two well-known names: the first is Commandant Bucquoy, who at the time when meticulous work was most needed, was one of the most active and persevering searchers for documentary truth. It was his hope to popularize, in the best sense of that word, the nascent science of the history of military uniforms. The hope was fulfilled: for his doctorate in 1908, he wrote and illustrated a thesis on "The Honor Guards of the First Empire," a model of its category. He then embarked upon the production of a series of

Above, left: THE SUTHERLAND HIGHLANDERS. *Private of 93rd Regiment in dress uniform, 1854;* Above, right: THE ROYAL SCOTS. *A private of the battalion company, 1742.* Below: THE ROYAL SCOTS GREYS. *Standard-bearer of the North British Dragoons, in field uniform, 1812. (Museum of Edinburgh Castle.)* ▶

three thousand color pictures, of postcard size, entitled "The Uniforms of the First Empire." For this series he enlisted, during a program that he brought to conclusion despite the intervention of two wars, the services of the best military artists in France and abroad.

Deeply distressed by the failure, in 1920, of Fallou's *La Giberne* (The Cartridge Pouch), the only publication then concerned with military uniforms, Commandant Bucquoy joined forces with artists and collectors in Strasbourg to found *Le Passepoil* (Piping), a publication that was devoted to the French Army, its uniforms, and its armament. Although for some thirty years his best efforts were devoted to that enterprise, he nevertheless found time to write two outstanding works: *The Uniforms of the French Army* (1938), with which were incorporated twenty-five watercolors, and *Fanfare and Music for Mounted Troops.* He enjoyed the collaboration of the finest military artists, who outdid themselves in honor of one of our best, and best-informed mentors.

The other man to whom we are indebted is Lucien Rousselot, who was discovered by Paul Armont. An accomplished illustrator, Rousselot has continued to turn out work that has placed collectors deeply in his debt; his name is associated with almost everything that has been published during the past three decades. During the dark days of the Occupation, Rousselot started *The French Army: Its Uniforms, Its Armament and Its Equipment.* That work comprises a number of two-page color spreads, each accompanied by a four-page text that is a model of brevity, precision, and learning.

For twenty years, without slackening his pace, Lucien Rousselot has persevered in a work for which no equivalent can be found elsewhere. His paintings, combining elegance of subject, precision of detail, and fidelity of color, have been accepted by collectors of figurines as "perfect models." Long may he live! His knowl-

edge, acquired through extensive and sometimes discouraging research, can thus be made available to the collectors of today and tomorrow.

This quick scanning of resources may serve as a measure of the forward progress made by many unassuming men, whose sole reward has been profitless, and somewhat tardy, praise.

Worthy of mention, also, are the unremitting and successful endeavours of the clubs in which

collectors are united throughout the world. Each of them issues a periodical publication that keeps its readers abreast of additions to international bibliography, and at the same time includes manifold studies, illustrated when the subject matter permits, on obscure or disputed aspects of the history of the military uniform.

The diminutive figurine, standing only a few inches high, has since its birth engendered an incredible amount of work—a tremendous, still increasing stack of books and periodicals.

There has been constant increase, too, in the number of collectors, who in their eagerness for information now comprise a clientele large enough to justify new editions of rare and original documents that were formerly confined to specialized libraries and hence not accessible to the general public.

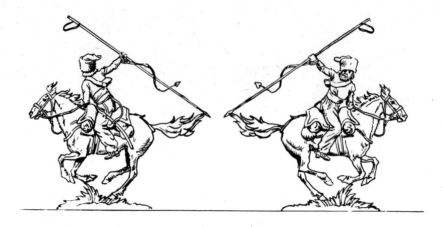

THREE-DIMENSIONAL COLLECTORS' ITEMS

The solid, or three-dimensional, military figurine, originally known simply as a lead soldier, was, as we have seen, nothing more than a toy, whereas the flat tin figurine, having already been granted its letters of nobility, was elevated to the rank of a collector's item.

Some critics of the former objected that its small size forced the most skillful of workers in miniature to eliminate certain details in the quest for an acceptable overall effect—which, it may be noted, was almost always attained. Others took exception to the capricious use of two facial aspects, not unlike that of ancient Egyptian engravings, in which a man could be represented either in full face or in profile. A three-quarters view inevitably exaggerated more faults than it corrected.

Still, it must be remembered that the most attractive boxes of lead soldiers, despite the research involved in their preparation, were conceived not to please the least particular or the least enlightened of collectors, but to appeal to juvenile purchasers.

The very density of the metal employed seems to have fostered the creation of a heavy, massive soldier for whom only conventional attitudes were possible. Nevertheless, there were buyers for every novel form that appeared on the market. Exportation, chiefly to transatlantic customers, enabled the manufacturers annually to bring out new models, which were well received because they were concerned for the most part with the armies of foreign nations.

Ronde-bosse[1] figurines as collectors' items seemed destined to commercial failure because of the times and the circumstances under which they were brought forth—namely, in Paris under the German occupation of 1940 to 1944. France at that time was lacking in raw materials and tin was utterly unobtainable. (The flat figurine makes no extravagant demand. For it, a few grams of metal suffice.) But, everything considered, the conditions of life then prevailing —the long evenings under the study lamp, and the need to accomplish something—were favor-

[1] *Ronde-bosse* is the sculptor's term for a figure that is fully three-dimensional, as opposed to a work in high relief.

SWEDISH CAVALRY OF THE EIGHTEENTH CENTURY. *Height 40 mm. By Eriksson. (Philippot Collection, Paris.)*

able to meditation, study, and patient research.

It was shortly before Christmas in 1942 that visitors to a modest exhibit of figurines in a large department store on the Right Bank had the pleasant surprise of seeing something entirely new. Was the favorable response due to the size scale, to the unusually realistic bearing, or to the three-dimensional appeal of the figurines? Whatever the reason, the public, both amateur and connoisseur, was enraptured by that display of figurines. The subjects were not petrified "at attention": they seemed to be alive. The lansquenet clothing designed by Alexandre Ballada no longer was an integral

GRENADIER OF THIRD DUTCH REGIMENT OF THE IMPERIAL GUARD *(large figurine). Height 20 cm. By G. Fouillé.* GRENADIER *(small figurine). Height 20 mm. By Alymer.*

part of the statuette. The garments draped a body that could be divined beneath them.

True, the new figurines could only be described as entertaining, but they nevertheless were a revelation. Upon close observation it was seen that the seams in sleeves and pantaloons were not imitations: the designer had been inspired to cut out, and to solder together, very thin sheets of lead. Plumed hats were placed on, rather than molded as a part of, the head. The plume itself was separately mounted, with a drop of solder. Yes, the beard still seemed artificial, but even that detail was to receive attention later. Two-handed swords, halberds, and daggers were now cast separately, all in appropriate scale. The cloak of the beer bibber, carelessly thrown over his shoulder, was formed from a separate sheet of lead.

Alexandre Ballada was not content to stop there. As an accomplished goldsmith who had spent many years at the bench, and who was skilled in the manipulation of forceps, files, and soldering torch, he had other surprises in store.

With the co-operation of his friend Robert Saintoin, he proceeded to develop realistic infantrymen at rest and on the march, cavalrymen and their steeds, all of which had been meticulously designed to scale by Lucien Rousselot, who frequently served as technical adviser.

From the original models, statuettes of plaster were made. From these plaster forms, in turn, were made molds, each of which was then checked by the engraver and an inspector. The heads, and the innumerable types of headdress, were of course cast separately. Horses presented a difficult problem, because their trappings varied with the service arm as well as with the period represented. Saddles, shabracks of sheepskin or cloth, and demishabracks, each required a separate mold.

Should the horses be represented as standing, walking or trotting? After some days of study, Ballada found the answer. With his jeweller's saw he deliberately dismembered the steed, on which the sculptor had already made uncounted corrections. He now had seven equine components that fitted perfectly together. For each part a separate mold was made.

Thus, by a clever selection of combinations, he could contrive horses standing or walking

in a dozen different attitudes; horses trotting at seven or eight distinct paces; horses galloping with five or six varying strides. For the first time there was a prancing cavalry, to replace the animals so accurately described by Christian-Gérard as "calves baptised as horses." Those nondescript beasts had admittedly been one of the reasons for the low esteem in which *ronde-bosse* subjects were held by serious collectors.

For the ordinary collector, the cost of making figurines by the new technique was well-nigh prohibitive. That problem was neatly solved by Robert Saintoin, who decided that separate components should be made available, at reasonable prices, to club members who could then, with their soldering irons, assemble their own infantrymen, cavalrymen, and horses.

Truth to tell, the first experiments undertaken by some of the bolder tinkerers were not remarkably successful. To guide their hands there was no "how-to" manual, because the full technique had yet to be developed. Yet some intrepid amateurs who were endowed with manual dexterity did achieve professional skill. Among them, Dr. André Hugo, an expert molder and accomplished painter, mastered the soldering iron, made light of many difficulties, and boldly undertook a series of "Knights of the Golden

Fleece." For that project he created complicated tournament helmets and draped his horses with caparisons that he painted with great dexterity. The fact that, after a few years, he abandoned the figurine in favor of small-scale models must have deprived us of many magnificent exhibits.

At about the same time, Auger, who carved his own molds, prepared a series of standard bearers of the Louis XVI-to-Revolution days whose realistic banners seem to flap in the wind.

Alexandre, the skillful painter who long worked for Paul Armont, was intrigued by the new production techniques and, addressing himself to the days of Louis XIII, re-created the little world of the Pont Neuf with subjects both colorful and lifelike. Another military painter of acknowledged talent, Eugène Leliepvre, quickly achieved success with *ronde-bosse* figurines, bringing forth trumpeters and kettledrummers that are breath-taking in their verisimilitude.

Some months after the liberation of Paris, in November 1944, the Society of Collectors

FIRST SWISS REGIMENT OF THE IMPERIAL ARMY, *1809.*
By Métayer. (Keller Collection, Paris.)

of Historical Figurines (whose name, it will be noted, no longer implies a limitation to lead soldiers) opened its ninth exposition at the Cognacq-Jay Museum. The atmosphere of that opening will not be forgotten by any of those who attended, and the display marked a turning point that should be emphasized. Only in Paris —after four years of shortages and suffering, with furious battles still raging in Alsace—could one have experienced that miracle of ingenuity in which, with the best of taste, technique and art were wedded.

The official inauguration was held under the auspices of General of the Armies Kœnig, who at the time was military governor of Paris. Present also was the fine arts director of the city, together with personages of importance in both the army and the world of arts and letters. It was a triumph.

It was, likewise, a revelation for the general public, which, in that setting of elegance, gained its first real knowledge of the figurine. Never before had collections of tin soldiers,

skillfully decorated by artists of renown, been exhibited in related groups. The tin figurine, there displayed on board mounts or in diorama, had attained a status it would be difficult to surpass. Conception, fidelity of execution, variety of background, left little to be desired. With very minor exceptions that judgment is confirmed after a lapse of more than fifteen years.

So successful was the novel in-the-round conception that any relationship to the lead soldier of earlier days was obliterated. The indisputable evidence of the new order of things was accepted by both tyro and expert.

While this is not the moment to engage in extended retrospection, it will bear repeating that the exposition was a significant milestone. It also seems proper to recall the names of some of the pioneers in a method of artistic expression that was destined first to establish a school, and then to be universally adopted.

Above: THE PUBLIC LETTER WRITER. *Ronde-bosse figurines by Alexandre. Height, 55 mm.* Below: ON LE PONT NEUF. *Personages of the time of Louis XIII—beggar, tinker, knife-grinder and peddler of ribbons. Ronde-bosse figurines by Alexandre. Height 55 mm. (Philippot Collection, Paris.)* ▶

There was Alexandre Ballada, who has already
been mentioned. His idea of casting components
separately was a most important factor in the
success enjoyed by *ronde-bosse* figurines, because
it enabled many beginning collectors to obtain
stocks of basic parts. Among the followers
deeply indebted to him were: Durand-Grimaldi,
Alexandre, André Hugo, Jacques Bittard, and
many others.

In due course, there appeared another in-
novation, *ronde-bosse* figurines manufactured
expressly for collectors. After long and careful
study of the problem, Mme. F. Métayer developed, from drawings made by Lucien Rousselot,
the first examples of her "Little Soldiers of
France", a series initially devoted to the First
Empire. Success was assured at the very outset
by the care bestowed on every detail of mold
making, casting, and assembly, and by the wis-
dom of Fernande Métayer, a painter whose
work has stood the test of time.

Mme. Métayer, also the founder of a school,
has made it easy for imitators, in France and
particularly in other lands, to follow the path
she has blazed. And in thus engendering what
might politely be called "tardy inspiration", there
lies, it would seem, the very accolade of success.

It is at this time that figurine makers became
fascinated with "individualism," ever an important factor in artistic achievement. There
developed a recognized urge to create a thing
that was different, or at least different in form,
from the work of one's colleagues.

Pierre Alexandre, who had long concentrated
on the delicate task of painting tin soldiers
for Paul Armont, revealed aptitudes that had
little in common with such precise work. He

GRENADIERS OF THE ARMIES OF PRUSSIA AND HANOVER,
*Eighteenth century. Extra large, ronde-bosse figures by
Stadden. (Mathiot Collection, Chantilly.)*

LANSQUENETS. *By A. Ballada. Height 55 mm. (Philippot Collection, Paris.)*

was intrigued by the people of the seventeenth century; not by members of the Royal Court, but by the inhabitants of the Court of Miracles; by the colorful and rowdy world of the Pont Neuf—bums and buffoons.

His favorite source books may well have been the volumes illustrated with so much spirit and animation by Abraham Bosse, the engraver who was a pupil of Callot. Thus was inspired the humorous series now in the Philippot Collection, including the tooth-puller and his companion the drummer, whose long rolls drowned out the screams of the patient; the barber plying his trade in the open air; the cobbler crouched in his tub; the public letter writer ensconced, like Diogenes, in his barrel-shelter; the scissors grinder; the fraudulent beggar; the tinker with a rack of kitchen utensils just collected from his customers; the vendor of ribbons. Their name is legion; their aspect barbarous. Would that they could all be enumerated! There is the physician, in pointed cap, followed by his associates—the pharmacist, the

giver of enemas, the surgeon, the crier of death with his bell; there is the notary with his clerks, and the public singer. All of them have been brought forth without too much attention to minor detail—but what color, what a feeling of life!

If the general public immediately accepted *ronde-bosse* figurines, there were at least a few collectors of long experience whose response was somewhat more reserved. Despite the indisputable evidence of the progress that had been made since the days of the original solid soldier, the conservatives believed that the tin figurine was, and would remain, *the* collector's item. They held that after a momentary popularity the latecomers would ever remain in the minority.

In the years that followed, there was an undeclared but tacitly admitted quarrel between the Ancients and the Moderns. Each side defended its position with arguments that at times were specious. To understand that rivalry, of which I personally was never convinced, it now becomes necessary to compare the techniques favored by each clan.

TECHNIQUES

Since the fine points of industrial technique lie beyond the scope of this work, attention can here be given only to a brief résumé of the general procedures followed in the manufacture of different types of figurines.

In principle, the casting of a flat figurine involves the oldest and simplest of methods—the use of a hollow, or sunken, mold. The designer, having completed his preliminary research, and having decided upon the attitude and height of his subject, proceeds to production. With a pen, he draws both sides of the figurine on tracing paper, in the dimensions on which he has decided. The two sides, obviously, must register exactly, and that is assured by folding the tracing paper along a vertical axis. The design is then passed to the engraver, who transfers the tracing in reverse, to two slabs of black Thuringian slate that has been selected for fineness of grain and absence of imperfections. The surfaces of the slate blocks have been so dressed and polished as to assure perfect contact between them.

Then begins the long and delicate work of engraving, with foot-controlled lathes, electric milling machines, and old-time hand tools, including burins of all sizes and shapes. The engraver constantly checks his work with a mirror and wax, the wax enabling him to take repeated proofs as he progresses. No retouching is possible, and the depth of the mold must be held to a minimum. When the mold-cutting is completed, a foreman prepares the two slate blocks, which are fitted with guide pins to hold them in alignment during the casting operation. The final step is the making of influx channels, and of vents to permit the escape of air, which is driven out by the molten metal.

The mold is gradually brought to the optimum temperature, so that the alloy may flow into its recesses without cooling to a point that would result in incomplete or imperfect castings.

The founder's reputation for manual dexterity is well deserved, because the operation is one that can be done only by hand. The quality of the castings thus produced is a result of:

(1) the artistic worth of the original design; (2) the care and precision with which the mold is cut; (3) the precise registry of the two parts of the mold; (4) the careful proportioning of the metals that comprise the alloy; (5) the temperature of the molten metal, and of the mold.

When the castings have cooled, the flash and sprue are removed. The figurine is then checked to make sure it is truly vertical with respect to its base.

Then the casting goes to the painter, who applies a base coating that has a dual function: protecting the metal against oxidation, and providing a surface that readily accepts paint.

For mold-making the classical material, as has been said, is blocks of black slate, which is still favored in Germany. In recent years,

CATHERINE DE MEDICIS. *Ronde-bosse figurine by R. Zuber. (Philippot Collection, Paris.)*

A KNIGHT OF THE GOLDEN FLEECE. *Detail of the helmet of the King of Poland. By the author (Frache Collection, Paris.)*

that stone has been replaced by various metals —bronze, alloys of bronze, or aluminium-magnesium alloys of type AG. 5. Although metal molds give satisfactory results, their rapid warm-up during the casting operation affects both the temperature and the fluidity of the molten metal.

For *demi-ronde-bosse* figurines (which might more accurately be styled "imitation *ronde-bosse*", the technique employed is substantially the same as for flat figurines. Because the cutting is necessarily much deeper, metal molds are generally used. The alloy is almost identical with that of printer's type, namely lead containing 20 to 25 per cent of antimony.

Ronde-bosse figures involve a much more complex procedure. At the outset the sculptor, relying upon documentation that shows or describes all sides of his subject, makes a full-scale model, whose height, not including the headdress, is approximately 55 mm. That model may be of wax, plaster of Paris, or—ideally when the subject is intricate—ivory. In most instances, heads, arms, and accessories require separate models, and hence separate molds.

When completed and approved, the model goes to the mold-cutter, who prepares a mold that may consist of two, three or four parts. Those parts are given to an artisan who equips them with guide pins and then cuts the sprue channels and air vents. He also provides a harness, to which the foundryman's work-handle may subsequently be attached. Finally, the mold-maker, with an eye on the original designs and the progress proofs, corrects any minor discrepancies. The mold is then ready for quantity production.

For toys, the model-maker bears in mind the advantage of a two-piece mold from which the figurine may be cast, complete, in a single operation. In any event, the number of accessory parts involving expensive hand labor is held to a minimum.

Conversely, limitless care is lavished upon figurines expressly intended for collectors. Both sculptor and engraver pay close attention to the smallest details: the drape of the garments, lapels and their buttons, sleeve ornaments, shoulder straps and epaulets, belts, coat and jacket pockets, leggings, and field boots with their cuffs and spurs. The characteristic ornamentation on helmets, shakos, and caps is reproduced. For each of those elements, which are often cast in duplicate, a separate mold is made. Thus, for the First Empire alone, more than two dozen molds are required!

It takes different molds to depict the infantryman at rest, at attention, on the march or running. Furthermore, he may be dressed in pantaloons or in knee britches with high or low gaiters. The mounted soldier may, in

Above: JOUSTING KNIGHTS. *Flat figurines. Height 65 mm. Arms and helmet visors are articulated. By Besold, circa 1835. (Focke Collection, Leverkusen.)* Below: THE TRAIN FROM NUREMBURG TO FURTH. *Early XIXth Century. Length, 40 cm. (Harms Collection, Hamburg.)* ▶

accordance with his branch of the service, wear cuffed, Hungarian, or dragoon-style riding boots.

As we have said, Alexandre Ballada was the first to perfect a realistic horse. Theoretically, that result was obtained by selection from seven molds—head and withers, body, legs, and tail —to which must be added the mold for the base. The sculptor makes alternative models of the body, with shabrack or demi-shabrack of sheepskin or cloth, saddles of various models, and saddlecloths of panther skin. He fashions various styles of cantle packs for greatcoats: round, square, and square with folded coat held under straps. The bearing and gait of his horses can be varied realistically by skillfully combining the forequarters and hind-quarters from some eighteen new molds. The attitude of head and neck must also be subject to change, to show a neck outstretched, a head raised, a mane blowing in the wind. For that purpose, a new series of supplementary molds was manufactured.

Now, when that multitude of cast parts has been classified and arranged, there comes the task of assembling them. As the solderer, after trimming away the flash, puts the parts together,

the steed slowly begins to take shape. There is a rider in the saddle; a hussar is ready to charge, pelisse slung over his left shoulder and sword-knot of his saber looped around his wrist.

Then, if the action may be so expressed, the painter takes the floor.

It is not easy to assess the expenditures involved in developing a quality product without skimping any single step, from the preliminary art work by a well-known military painter down to the choice of a humble assembler whose deft soldering iron may leave no visible trace.

And nothing has been said of the manifold accessories without which there could be no soldier. For him there must be available haver-sacks and cartridge pouches, canteens, kit bags, and drums, as well as swords and bayonets of designs that, because they vary with time, are not interchangeable.

Clearly, such an enterprise calls for financial preparations, considerable capital investment, and a crew of technicians competent to turn out in quantity finished products that will appeal to customers always eager for novelties. Thus it is that the few producers of figurines

Far left: BRITISH LIFEGUARD, *1812;* next left: TWO SWISS GUARDS. *Height 20 mm. By Alymer, of Valencia;* center: TWO SWISS SAPPERS. *By Metayer. Height 55 mm.;* right: BRITISH INFANTRYMEN, *1812. (Keller Collection, Paris.)*

for collectors quite understandably give their attention, at the outset, to the First Empire— because the first purchase of the beginning collector, regardless of his nationality, is a grenadier of the Imperial Guard. Then comes Napoleon, ahorse or on foot, followed, as circumstances permit, by some of his marshals, in bicorn hats and costumes embroidered in gold. And one *must* have Marshal Murat, the Murat of the hundred dazzling uniforms.

With that general staff organized, the collector then makes his choice of light-horsemen— lancers, hussars, or carabineers. Thus little by little, the principal actors of the days of empire are gathered together.

The makers of toy soldiers, often collectors themselves, can scarcely be criticized, when one realizes the risks involved in their ambitious

AN INDIAN ENCAMPMENT. *Flat figurines by Loy, painted and decorated by Mathiot. (Mathiot Collection, Chantilly.)*

undertakings, for fostering the craze for that fascinating period of French history.

It should be added that, whereas the tin soldier, small in size and low in price even when well executed, tempted the amateur to buy a given model in quantity, a single *ronde-bosse* figurine was sufficient unto itself, as a prototype. The latter had all the qualities of a small statue. The owner, holding it delicately by the base, could study it on all sides before placing it, as an object of unquestioned decorative effect, on a bookshelf or in a showcase.

Precisely those reflections have been made by some of my collector friends who have confidentially lamented the fact that similar honor has not been paid to lesser-known subjects of equal interest and worth. And so saying, they manipulate parts that, after assembly, are destined to become a voltigeur or a light cavalry-man. At the same time, imagination tells them what should be added, or filed away, to turn

the subject into a musketeer of the time of Louis XIII, or a bodyguard for Charles X.

Of necessity, they have become adept in the use of the soldering iron. Sad experience has proved that the quick soldering used on the cheaper commercial articles is incompatible with precision work. In the absence of any popular manual on "Ways and Means of Making Figurines," they proceed by trial and error, with a perserverance their friends call stubbornness. Then, after frequent failures, comes the day when, with manifest pride, they succeed in soldering together two pieces of tin plate to form the skirt of a garment. The thing may be as stiff as the snout of a teapot, but it is free-standing and distinct from the mass of metal that represents the trousers.

They are now on the right track, and they cannot be halted!

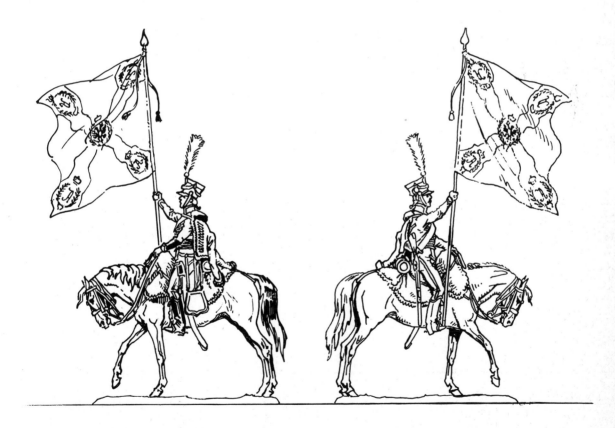

TROPHIES OF AUSTERLITZ. *Front and back of a flat tin figurine. Illustration considerably enlarged. By Rousselot. (Rousselot Collection, Paris.)*

THE MODEL SOLDIER

The ultimate goal of the persistent figurine enthusiast is to create a model—a model that need not be revised, in so far as shape and attitude are concerned. That is why, for the kind of figurine with which we are now concerned, I like the English term "Model Soldier" (which in two words says as much as the French can say in four).

The long hours devoted to the development of the model are not counted. Nothing counts but the result.

Instead of starting with a subject that is preconceived to the last detail, but from which inappropriate parts must be eliminated, why not make, once and for all, a sort of manikin

Above, left: OHIO NATIONAL GUARD. *Sergeant standard-bearer in winter uniform, 1909;* Above, right: HORSEMAN OF FIRST CITY TROOP. *Cleveland, 1877. Height, 36 mm.* Below, left: BUGLER OF FIRST CITY TROOP. *Cleveland, 1877;* Below, right: HORSEMAN OF FIRST CITY TROOP. *Dress uniform, 1881. By Berdou. (Thoburn Collection, Cleveland.)* ►

—a torso with two definitely separate legs, similar to the small model of the human body that enables an artist to visualize any desired pose? Like an unclothed doll, the manikin can then be dressed as fancy dictates. With a jeweler's saw, one can free a leg from the base on which it is resting, articulate the calf of that leg, and separate the trunk from the body so it may be placed, and soldered, in the desired position. Thus may the feeling of life be given to an inanimate form.

BARON LEJEUNE. *By Leliepvre, after a self-portrait. (Mathiot Collection, Paris.)*

THE FARRIER. *Horse grenadiers, 1745. After a painting by Lenfant. By Leliepvre. (Mathiot Collection, Chantilly.)*

To that end, special materials must be prepared. A set of tinsmith's rollers will produce thin strips of lead varying in thickness, in accordance with the intended application, from 0.4 to 1 mm. From that kind of fabric, which is to be soldered rather than sewn, articles of clothing will be cut, in accordance with carefully prepared templates. Experience will dictate by how much the waist of the model must be reduced to accept the multiple thicknesses with which it will be draped. Trousers, built up from thin sheets of lead, will reveal the knee and the turn of the calf. Fabric folds need not be simulated—they will appear where they belong—and sleeves and their ornaments will look natural. The greatcoat, if tailored to a rather loose fit, will be gracefully draped, perhaps with one side thrown over the shoulder as if by a gust of wind. Pleats and large folds may be fashioned with the aid of surgical forceps.

Each new model invites the perfection of a technique not previously essayed, the invention of an intriguing detail: the tresses of the hussar,

CAVALRY OFFICER UNDER LOUIS XIII. *Miniature manikin. Height 40 cm. (Scale, 1.5: 10) Over his cloth coat the rider wears a cuirass with brassarts and with splint-armor cuisses of blued steel. Ornaments are of gilded copper. Cuirass, helmet with neck-guard, and sword by Rocheron, a specialist. Horse and rider by Leliepvre. (Mathiot Collection, Chantilly.)*

formed from fine brass wire and held under the shako by a drop of solder, stream backward as his steed gallops ahead. So do the sleeves of his dolman.

STANDARD-BEARER OF THE CARIGNAN-SALLIÈRES REGIMENT. *Circa 1666. (Subsequently known as "Soissons".) Here shown in French uniform. For campaigning in the snows of Canada, where moccasins and snowshoes were worn, the hat was replaced by a fur cap. Made and painted by Desfontaines.*

CHARLES VI IN HUNTING COSTUME. *From a series of kings. By the author. (Frache Collection, Paris.)*

From thin sheets of brass, one cuts straps for the cartridge pouch, reins, sword belts, sabretache straps, and rifle slings. The same metal sheet will be used to fashion the body of a drum, which will then be fitted with hoops of thick lead, snares of fine wire and tension keys of thin lead. On a jeweler's anvil it is a simple matter to hammer out a curved saber for the light cavalryman, or to form the hussar's straight saber, whose scabbard rings are wound from the brass wire used for the hilt and the sword guard. The hat, cut from lead in the flat, as though the material were felt, is fitted to the wearer's head, cocked slightly over one eye, and adorned with a plume. As for hair styles, there are at least five or six different ones, ranging from thick locks formed by successive applications of the soldering iron, to the "dog's ears" of the Revolutionary period, the catogan, and the "pigeon's wing" mode of the time of Louis XV.

Skillful application of the engraver's burin will reshape an ear or the arch of an eyebrow, because tooling, too, evolves, little by little, in response to one's ever-increasing demands for a perfected technique. The modus operandi, moreover, takes on an individual style, which,

like that of a painter, identifies the craftsman.

The preferred workbench is, like that of a jeweler or an engraver, a solid block of oak so cut away at the front that the forearms may rest squarely on it, to steady the hands during delicate operations. On the bench there will be two or three electric soldering irons, of different wattage; a jeweler's anvil with small hammers and saws; and files of many shapes and sizes. The files should be chromium-plated because lead, surprisingly, is an exceedingly difficult metal to work. Necessary also is an assortment of forceps, including the kind used by surgeons, as well as a pin-vice to serve as the oft-required third hand.

Last but not least is an assortment of solders, indispensable because the worker lays down his file only to pick up a soldering iron. The solders must be low in lead content. Most popular is the bismuth solder, consisting of equal parts of tin, lead, and bismuth. For extremely fine work, there is a cadmium solder whose very low melting point recommends it for fashioning a cockade, a decoration, the catch

PHARAMOND RAISED ON THE SHIELD AND PROCLAIMED KING OF THE FRANKS. *After an engraving by Philippoteaux. By the author. (Frache Collection, Paris.)*

of a cartridge pouch, or a knot of ribbon. Soldering is the fundamental operation in assembling a plurality of parts, which must be added, one at a time, in a very definite sequence. Lace at the wrist must go on before the cuff of the glove which, in turn, must precede the cuff of the uniform sleeve. One moment of carelessness and all is lost! Solder is also, like the sculptors pellets of clay, a basic framework material. As the clay is dressed with a roughing chisel, solder is worked down with a file. No preliminary step is more important to the final result than careful modeling, upon which depend both style and bearing.

It was a technique akin to that just described that enabled Lacomblez to create for the Deconinck Collection in Brussels, the amazing Incas and Aztecs that we are privileged to reproduce here. A decade ago, one could not have foreseen anything duplicating the quality of those *ronde-bosse* exhibits. They reflect serious research in

CONSTABLE DUGUESCLIN. *With the royal sword. The first of a series of "Constables and Marshals of France." By the author.*

AN OFFICER OF THE PACIFIC COMPANY. *Circa 1698. After a water color by Rousselot. (By, and in the Collection of Desfontaines.)*

CAVALRY TROPHIES. *A horseman of the Tenth Hussars brings back a British infantry flag. Spanish Campaign of 1811. By the author. (Frache Collection, Paris.)*

some twenty source books, in different languages, and likewise reveal incomparable virtuosity on the part of the artist. Lacomblez made light of problems as difficult as they were unusual.

There lies proof, if proof were needed, that nothing is impossible for today's exponents of the *ronde-bosse* figurine. There, too, is the handsomest answer to its detractors of yesteryear.

BREAKING IN THE HORSE. *Morning on the race track. By Leliepvre. (Mathiot Collection, Chantilly.)*

PAINTING

A survey of the procedures employed in the production of figurines would hardly be complete without some comment on painting, of which, however, we will consider only the technical aspects.

Does the painting of a *ronde-bosse* figurine differ from that of a flat one? The answer is Yes.

In a tin figurine of standard dimensions, there is no relief. However, the older pieces, which had a height of eight, ten or even twelve centimeters, were correspondingly thicker, and therefore exhibited more pronounced modeling. But the engraving served merely to define the limits of, rather than to create, the relief. The vest, jacket, and greatcoat, superimposed on the same figurine, did not actually consist of separate masses of metal.

To differentiate between those garments was the responsibility of the painter, who achieved that end by methods substantially like those he would have employed in oil painting, albeit sometimes in reverse sequence. To be more explicit, instead of beginning with light tints that would later contrast with a light-to-dark gamut of shadows, he generally started with the darker tones, thus emphasizing the engraver's tool strokes. He then turned to lighter and lighter colors, and at times terminated his work with a subtle touch of almost pure white. Both light and shade were enhanced either by the use of paint to which a colorless varnish had been added, or when detail would have been obscured through such thickening, by covering the entire figurine, as soon as it was thoroughly dry, with a thin film of varnish. Examine a good photograph, in color or black and white, of a figurine after the painting operation. If it has some of the three-dimensional effect normally associated with high relief, the painting was properly done.

Now scrutinize, in a good light, a *ronde-bosse* figurine that has received only the priming coat that must precede the application of paint. When you rotate the figurine slowly, you will observe a natural formation of shadows which change as the model is turned and which, when motion is stopped, assume still different values. In that respect, the figurine resembles a statue—from which, in fact, it differs only in size.

It would therefore be futile and wrong, in view of the classical "three dimensions" that define perfect mass, to simulate arbitrarily and in conventional fashion, the shadows that will fall where they belong under any given lighting. The conclusion is obvious. What is needed, rather than painting for effect, is a precise rendering of matte colors, enhanced by diluents that impart a normal appearance to the fabrics being portrayed. Brilliant spots of color are

THE CURVET. *Originating in the elaborate horsemanship of the eighteenth century, the curvet comprises a series of prancing leaps during which the forefeet do not touch the ground. Still taught in Vienna. By Leliepvre. (Mathiot collection, Chantilly.)*

THE FIRST CONSUL. *In his crimson coat, with gold embroidery. A magnificent piece of work by Berdou. (Philippot collection, Paris.)*

used only for boots, polished leather, and of course for gold lace and such metallic pieces as side arms, buttons, and trimmings.

If the flat-figurine enthusiast has neither the ambition nor the skill necessary for the work in miniature that the embellishment of the tin soldier requires, he should seek the aid of a qualified artist who will be able to produce a collector's item incorporating the three basic essentials: good design, good engraving, and expert painting.

In almost every instance, those who develop *ronde-bosse* collections paint the master models with their own hands, and carefully inspect all copying entrusted to others, so that any error or unjustified whim may be corrected.

It is with good reason that the producers of model soldiers invariably do their own painting. After deciding upon the bearing and stance of the subject, they have painstakingly assembled the model, piece by piece; they cannot leave to others the interpretation of a costume to

which they have devoted a long and difficult research. If they decide not to show in relief a given detail of that garment, there is a good reason: knowing that the detail would be lost under a coat of paint, they reserve the right eventually to highlight it with a deft touch of the brush. To cite but one example: the metal ornament at the center of a gorget may be represented by a very small drop of solder, but a spot of silver paint against the gold background will have the same appearance, with the identical feeling of relief.

Here I would like to dispose of two frequently advanced assertions that I consider pleasant paradoxes. A man of experience, who speaks with authority where figurines are concerned, asserts with evident sincerity that "to do a good job of painting a *ronde-bosse* figurine, it is better not to know how to paint." But who would entrust to untutored hands the assignment of embellishing a horseman upon which three or four days of labor have been expended? Not I. And I am confident that Mlle Desfontaines, whom I consider to be one of the cleverest and most accomplished of figurine painters, would unhesitatingly agree with me.

Then there are the impatient folk who rush through the process of assemblage without troubling to pick up a file to remove the last trace of solder, or to efface the mark of a careless tool. They smilingly assure you that a coat of paint will take care of all that. But paint does not correct or camouflage anything. What is worse, painting emphasizes slipshod work and accentuates mistakes.

Know-how, while not a substitute for talent, does eliminate mediocrity, and that is why the collector prefers competent craftsmanship to poor painting.

NOTABLES EN ROUTE TO MONTEZUMA. *Pre-Columbian civilization. Height, not including headgear, 55 mm. By Lacomblez, after documentation by Deconinck. (Deconinck collection, Brussels.)* ▶

SCALE MODELS AND DIORAMAS

The original diorama is generally conceded to be the one that was set up in Paris between 1820 and 1840 by Daguerre, the photographer, and Bouton. It was on display at the Place du Château d'Eau, which is today the Place de la République.

If this large-scale representation was something new—its success was destined to bring forth many imitations which were called "panoramas" —the idea was not. As proof of that assertion, one may cite two dioramas that were exhibited at the Army Museum, and skillfully and successfully peopled with lead figurines. The oldest is one that represents the Battle of Dettingen, so-called from the Bavarian hamlet situated a few miles southeast of Hanau, in Lower Franconia. There, on June 27, 1743, British Field Marshal J. Dalrymple (Earl of Stair), in the presence of his sovereign George II, won a victory over the French armies commanded by Marshal de Noailles. The exhibit, measuring 18 by 52 inches, shows the winding course of the river Main, whose right bank is a rugged terrain of groves, woods, and steep hillsides. Across the plain bordering the left bank are encampments—rows of painted lead tents cast in long, saw-toothed strips. Roads meander between the tent rows, and batteries of artillery face each other from opposite sides of the river.

The lines of miniature combattants, standing shoulder to shoulder, are, like the tents, cast in continuous strips, the height of the infantry being about 6 mm. and that of the cavalry from 11 to 12 mm. The opposing forces are distinguished only by color—red for the English, blue for the French. The representation of villages and towns is somewhat schematic, and houses, churches, and fortifications are not in proportionate scale. Place names, troop movements and their points of departure are shown by flat markers. A handwritten sign, bearing the Noailles coat of arms, announces that: "The survey of the battle was made by Le Seigne, then General of the Engineers and subsequently Engineer in Charge of Constructions for the King, under whose supervision the model was made in 1787 by a former guards officer."

The second and more ambitious diorama, measuring about 50 by 67 inches, is of much greater importance from the viewpoint of documentation, history, and artistic accomplishment. It shows the Battle of Lodi, as fought on May 10 and 11, 1796, and it was executed in 1804 by the elder Boitard (Martin) "on the orders of the First Consul, to commemorate the battle fought on the 21st of the month Floréal, in the Year IV." Here we have a true scale model in toises,[1] at a ratio of 1:144, that is exceptional in composition and in execution.

It may be appropriate briefly to review the situation on the eve of the Battle of Lodi. After the victories at Montenotte, Dego and Millesimo, the young commanding general of the army in Italy signed an armistice with the Austrians on April 28. Ten days later he was at Plaisance, while Beaulieu had fallen back on the Adda, a tributary of the Po. On May 10, the French troops pushed forward to Lodi, which was seized by the advance guard before the enemy could destroy the bridge leading to the town. Bonaparte forced the passage with a column of crack infantry, while his cavalry forded river the upstream. The mass of his infantry, debouching from the neighboring streets, surged forward in serried ranks, under the leadership of Masséna, Berthier, Lannes, and Reille. Crossing the bridge under a hail of bullets, the French pinned down the Austrian artillerymen at their guns. That operation, opening up Lombardy to the French forces,

CONFEDERATE TROOPS IN RETREAT AFTER THE BATTLE OF GETTYSBURG. *July 3, 1863. Detail of the center of a diorama. Height of figures in foreground, 15.5 cm. (West Point Museum.)*

◄

[1] Toise: an ancient measure of length, equal to 1.949 meters, or approximately 77 inches.

THE BATTLE OF HASTINGS. *Detail of left portion. King Harold, mortally wounded by an arrow in the eye, stands with his brothers Gurth and Leofwin. The diorama, measuring about 75 by 120 cm. is peopled with tin figurines from various sources. (Royal United Service Museum, London.)*

demoralized the Austrian Army, which beat a retreat to the Mincio River.

The center of the diorama shows the principal thoroughfare of the town, with its monumental sculptured gate. On either side, the network of streets and alleys is jammed with infantry. The tile-roofed houses are reflected in the stream, and those nearest to the bridge show the effects of bombardent by Beaulieu's

artillery, which, posted on the heights of the left bank, have poured direct and enfilading fire on the bridge. The French artillery is replying. The spire of one church is ablaze, and some of the enemy's fieldpieces are dismounted. Along the roads on the Austrian side of the river, the disorganized convoys are obviously under the fire of the French.

Would that I could depict the quality, delicacy, and realism of detail! After more than a century and a half, the colors of the houses, roofs, and landscape have retained the pastel tones characteristic of the Italian countryside. At the left of the bridge there is a marble statue whose base is surrounded by a grillwork that must be made from strands of horsehair. There stands Bonaparte, and drawn up on the river bank is a small boat that has been smashed by artillery fire. The whole scene teems with action: soldiers are on the run, entering and leaving the houses; cavalry advances at the gallop. Some fieldpieces are surrounded by their gun crews; others have been put out of action.

Most amazing is the fact that the infantrymen have a height of 10 mm and that the cavalry is only half again as high. A gun carriage has a length of 20 mm. The figurines have no bases: each piece is stuck into the ground by a small pin projecting downward from the leg of man or horse. The delicacy of the figurines *(demi-, or more accurately quart-ronde-bosse),* which were certainly cast in slate molds, and the malleability of the metal employed, combined to provide a feeling of life. By a deft use of forceps, a leg was bent forward or backward to suggest a walking or a running soldier. In the same way, the pace of a horse was demonstrated.

How many pieces comprise the whole? Hundreds, certainly. It is not possible to give an accurate estimate, but from no other exhibit, have I gained such an impression of crowds, of massed military formations. The horses hitched to caissons and supply waggons are harnessed with the broad wooden collars and bolsters that were then standard equipment. The traces are made from silk threads. Saddle horses are harnessed, in accordance with the arm of the service, with shabracks of sheepskin or cloth that were cut from tracing paper. The hussars, clad in dolmans and wearing shakos, have cartridge pouches and belts that are also made from paper. The French infantry, with shoulder straps crossing on the chest, sport service caps with drooping red plumes. Fieldpieces are fashioned from copper. Gun carriages and wagons of all kinds, together with their wheels, are cut from cardboard, pasted up, and painted.

Unfortunately the painting of the figurines was done with gouache, without protection from exposure to the atmosphere. Both infantry and cavalry have suffered from an incurable malady—lead sickness. Many have wasted away to a mere pinch of lead oxide; others would be wiped out if touched by the point of a lead pencil. Theoretically, it should be possible to re-place them, in a décor that is still intact, if each zone were first carefully photographed. Actually,

no one has dared to undertake a work of that magnitude, the cost of which would be difficult to estimate.

The quality of the exhibit is definitely a result of the professional accomplishments of the maker and his assistants. For the work, precise documentation was indispensable. The technical information was provided by an eyewitness, Bacler d'Albe, a young engineer in the Army

THE BATTLE OF HASTINGS. *October 14, 1066. Detail of right portion of diorama made by Otto Gottstein in London. The Norman cavalry of William the Conqueror, after feigning a retreat that enticed the Anglo-Saxons from their entrenchments, has about-faced and charged forward, supported by William's bowmen, who, from the heights, riddle Harold's troops with a shower of arrows. (Royal United Service Museum, London.)*

of the Republic who, having caught the eye of Napoleon at the siege of Toulon, was attached to the general staff as an artillery captain. That assignment he held throughout the Italian campaign of 1796, when he distinguished himself at Arcole. After the Peace of Campo Formio, he was commissioned to draw up a map of the campaign. The map consisted of fifty-four sheets!

He, like Lejeune, has left us realistic documents, because he was one of the very few reporters who, sketchbook in hand, lived through the Napoleonic campaigns. His watercolor, "The Crossing of the Bridge at Lodi," which hangs in the Ministry of War, is a scrupulous, three-dimensional reproduction that is highly accurate in detail. Equally remarkable are his watercolors of the battles of Arcole and Austerlitz.

After being promoted to brigadier general, Bacler d'Albe was placed at the head of the Quartermaster's Department, where he trained the artists attached to that ministry.

To conclude a study whose length, it is hoped, may be justified by its unusual character, it seems pertinent to ask one final question: why did Napoleon select for reproduction the Battle of Lodi, in preference to military engagements which, with the lapse of time, seem to be of much greater military importance? The answer is given by Napoleon himself, in his *Memorial of St. Helena:*

"...it was only after the Battle of Lodi that I recognized the possibility, after all, of becoming a decisive actor on our political stage. Then it was that the first spark of high ambition was kindled."

In fact after signing an armistice without authority from the Directory, whose coffers he had filled but which he so despised that he had decided not to obey its instructions any longer, Bonaparte did flatly refuse to carry out the order that a portion of his command be transferred to the aged Kellermann. Let them give him his way, and all of Italy will be conquered—already the solider had become a statesman. And that is why he willed to us the Lodi diorama.

Let us now return to Paris, to the Carnavalet Museum, for a look at Thiriot's most unusual "Scenic Perspective of the Seine," which could be studied with profit by many of today's makers of scale models. So skillful is the perspective that its effect is enhanced, rather than diminished, in the photographic reproduction. This model, made in 1817, is 38 inches wide and only 12 inches deep. It is constructed entirely of natural wood, including the human figures. The people in the foreground stand just 15 mm. high.

The view is that seen from the Place Dauphine. In the foreground is the Pont Neuf, with the base of the statue of Henry IV that was pulled down in 1792; it was not to be replaced until 1818. In the middle distance one sees the Pont des Arts, which leads to the Institute. This, the first iron bridge in Paris, was under construction from to 1802 to 1804, and was for many years adorned with tubs of orange trees, which the artist has included. Further down stream is the Pont Royal, which connects the Louvre, on the right, with the rue du Bac. The background includes the Pont de la Concorde, beyond the Tuileries terrace.

In the same museum there is another page from the history of France: "The Arrival of the Duke of Orleans at the Hôtel de Ville, on July 31, 1830." This important model, measuring some 60 by 80 inches, shows the Place de Grève as it then appeared, with its many shops. It is surrounded by ancient, gable roofed houses, bristling with chimneys. The Hôtel de Ville, designed by Le Boccador, was not completed until the end of the reign of Henry IV. It was destroyed by fire in 1871.

Louis-Philippe of Orleans who, following the ousting of Charles X, has been named Lieutenant General of the Kingdom, is seen arriving on horseback in uniform. He is escorted by the National Guard, bearing the tricolor that has just replaced the white flag of the Restoration. On the steps of the gate of honor stands Lafayette, who at the age of seventy-four and after thirty-five years of retirement, has again been named Commander of the National Guard. He is accompanied by Thiers and Lafitte and the municipal magistrates. Lafayette embraces the man who, on August 6, is to become the King of France, as Louis-Philippe I. The 20 mm. figurines, *demi-ronde-bosse,* are for the most part in civilian dress, in the style of those days. They are amusing little characters. Crowd

movements, adroitly suggested, impart a feeling of life to the scene.

At the Navy Museum in Paris and worthy of mention are two scale models, prepared with precision and fidelity, representing two important stages in the moving and setting up of the Luxor obelisk. That operation, undertaken in 1831, required not less than three months of labor. It engaged a multitude of workmen because it was necessary to dig a channel for the barge on which the pillar was transported. In this scene, the 15 mm. figurines, which seem microscopic in the midst of the quasi-desert landscape, have been specially executed in *demi-ronde-bosse*. The scene showing the erection of the obelisk in the Place de la Concorde features the apparatus that was contrived to accomplish what was for those days a veritable tour de force from the viewpoints of both calculation and application.

The fact that those operations were conceived and carried out by Lebas, a Navy engineer,

THE BRIDGES OF PARIS. *A graphic perspective of the Seine, as seen from the Place Dauphine. In the foreground, the Pont Neuf. Next, the foot bridge to the Institut, the Pont Royal, and, in the distance, the Pont de la Concorde. Entirely of unpainted wood, including the figurines. The diorama, made by Thiriot in 1817, is a model of perspective. (Carnavalet Museum, Paris.)*

explains why the two models are on display at the Palais de Chaillot, where the Navy Museum is now located.

It should be noted that the figurines described above are an instance of figurines expressly designed at a desired scale for predetermined and unusual use.

The growing popularity of tin soldiers, and of flat figurines developed for collections, has given many amateur collectors the idea of employing those standard pieces in making scale models with appropriate backgrounds. They find it much easier to reverse than to follow the procedure of the specialist.

It happens that the standard heights—30 mm. for pedestrians and 40 mm. for horsemen—

correspond rather closely to a scale of 1:55, which is entirely acceptable because it holds the terrain to reasonably proportioned dimensions. Almost every subject may be had in a wide variety of attitudes and, as has been seen, the possibilities may be multiplied by adroit manipulation.

So there now have blossomed forth a multitude of small tableaux, reproducing historical episodes of every description. Some amateur diorama builders are content with an harmonious grouping of several figurines whose unesthetic bases are concealed in an unevenly landscaped terrain where shrubs and trees abound. The background of the scene, however, is only suggested. A good example is "The Indian Encampment" (p. 48), which we have reproduced from the Mathiot collection.

THE BATTLE OF LODI (May 10, 1796). Detail seen from the left bank of the River Adda. The French troops debouch from the town that they have just captured and surge across the bridge, under a hail of bullets, to harass the Austrian army, commanded by Beaulieu. This remarkable scale model was executed by Boitard on the orders of the First Consul, who, during the battle, was stationed by the statue at the left of the bridge. (Army Museum, Paris.)

This conception has the advantage of reducing the required space to a minimum. Since the figurines are not bulky, a depth of a few centimeters is sufficient. Hence an exhibit of this kind can readily be housed in a show case.

Other amateurs, using only three or four figurines against a background painted on carboard or transparent material, achieve true relief tableaux of such shallow depth that they may be mounted under glass and hung on the wall.

But in most instances, the diorama conforms to the now familiar definition: an "open window" looking upon a realistic scene in which scale and atmosphere are attained by decoration, by the use of appropriate accessories and, above all, by expert lighting. The more nearly the "window" principle approaches the ideal of a distant view of a scene that seems wider than the opening, the more satisfactory is the effect. For the same reason, the backdrop should not be flat, like a curtain falling parallel to the protecting glass. It should be a panorama, with a concave curve, coupled to the right and left

sides of the façade in which the opening is cut. That façade is necessarily a broad frame.

While the true scale model involves small-scale construction of three-dimensional buildings and accessories that theoretically may be viewed from all sides, the diorama, with a foreground built to the scale of the figurines positioned there, must make maximum and scientific application of the art of perspective.

The difference between scale model and diorama is like that between a stage setting and a motion picture set. Such is the difference between the "Scenic Perspective of the Seine" and the "Bridge at Lodi," which we have already examined in detail.

To increase the feeling of depth (which is not only artificial but also out of scale), intermediate planes are positioned at decreasing distances, from front to back, as dictated by the nature of the terrain and the location of woods, walls, and buildings. In some cases, the height of trees or structures in the foreground may exceed the scale of the figurines. Both height and apparent volume then decrease rapidly—as do roadside rows of trees or telegraph poles—toward a vanishing point at the back of the exhibit.

It follows that, in a diorama, figurines must be placed in planes that are rather close together. When it is necessary to show people in the distance—e.g., enemy lines or columns of troops on the march—the figurines may be cut as silhouettes that are dark in tone, or they may be made smaller than the foreground figures. The spectator's impression of the site is influenced by the height of the horizon line, as well as by appropriate use of ascending, oblique, and descending perspective. Clever application of that principle was seen at a recent exhibition of figurines in Paris, in a very small diorama entitled "The Battle of Salamis." From the spectator's viewpoint, on the heights, the action took place far beneath him, in the distance.

Lighting, as has been intimated, emphasizes and enhances the atmosphere of the setting. Light is, in fact, an important element of décor.

Its color and intensity will vary with the nature of the countryside, season of the year, and hour of the day. Supplementary lights may be required to wipe out undesirable shadows, particularly those cast by midstage drops, or by some of the buildings, trees, and bridges.

Unwanted shadow may ruin the effect of the most carefully conceived perspective. This, of course, is not to say that all shadows are undesirable.

In general, the best illumination is obtained from footlights, or from tubular light sources placed perpendicularly or at an oblique angle to the clear glass front of the diorama. Several sources of medium intensity are always preferable to one or two very bright lights, since with the former, tonal qualities can be varied. All secondary lights should be located at a height adequate to insure good diffusion. A protective screen of ground glass should be placed between the light sources and the scene, in such a fashion as to provide ventilation, thus obviating all risk of damage from heat given off by the lights.

Makers of dioramas now enjoy the advantages of many new materials that yesterday were unknown, including a wide variety of plastics. They can even obtain semi-finished stage properties that can be modified in accordance with the requirements of the exhibit.

In Germany, where the tin soldier was born, the educational possibilities of the figurine were quickly recognized. It was instantly evident that tableaux made far greater appeal to the imagination than pictures in books. Considered singly, the tiny personages did not tell a story. When knowingly grouped, however, they could scarcely fail to arouse the interest of young people who found in them intriguing illustrations for school books that were often dull. Adults, also, were attracted by the artistic worth of such presentations.

A most spectacular demonstration was provided by the Leipzig Exposition of 1930. Organized with the efficiency that characterizes such enterprises on the far side of the Rhine, that exposition attracted specialists from many walks of life: directors of museums, leaders in the field of education, artists, and technicians. Its principal object successfully realized, the exhibit then became an important factor in national and international propaganda. More than one hundred and fifty tableaux were shown. The displays, grouped in accordance with their themes, covered the history of the world, man, antiquity, and the German people. All were devoted to episodes well calculated to awaken and foster national pride.

THE BATTLE OF DETTINGEN *(1743). Part of a diorama made in 1787. On the right bank of the Main, English troops, with cavalry on the right and left wings, are aligned under the fire of the artillery of Marshal Noailles, who is to be defeated by Count Stair, the British Field Marshal. This ensemble may be considered the progenitor of French dioramas. (Army Museum, Paris.)*

In 1931, a permanent figurine museum was established in the Plassenburg Castle, the former seat of the Hohenzollerns, at Kulmbach in Bavaria. During and after World War II, the museum was seriously damaged, and pillaged. But through the diligence of the local authorities and the co-operation of various collectors' clubs, it was completely restored. In 1953, on the occasion of an international congress, the organizers were able to present, in the medieval setting of large Gothic rooms, nearly one hundred and fifty new dioramas. The whole exhibit became an important attraction for the tourists who flock to that region.

The majority of those museum exhibits are restrained in conception, and very modern in style. They are characterized by high sky lines and very low horizons. The décor is suggested, rather than exactly delineated.

Hamburg is likewise a center for very active collectors, among whom should be mentioned M. Onken, Dr. Guinov, Karl Harms, and MM. Banthin and Baumgart—all renowned as creators of dioramas. Many of their interesting tableaux are concerned with the storied history of the old free city.

In the development of figurine tableaux, Austria closely followed the German lead. As early as 1909, the dean of Viennese collectors, Teuber-Weckersdorf, exhibited, during the anniversary of the 1809 Campaign, a diorama of the

TROOPS IN TRAINING. *The "Royal-des-Vaisseaux" regiment, 1760. Part of a diorama by Leliepvre, with figurines by Mme. Métayer. (Gritton Collection, Paris.)* ▶

Battle of Aspern. That imposing presentation covered some 430 square feet, and incorporated nearly 30,000 tin personages.

The same amateur, in 1930, showed "The Crossing of the Danube by Prince Eugene, at Belgrade, in 1717." That classical example of Austro-German tactics includes a considerable number of small craft, and 6000 figurines.

Among his worthy successors are Ludwig Gärtner, R. de Riedmatten, and Dr. Erich Kröner, all of whom are renowned alike for meticulous research, for excellent stage-setting, and for painting of high quality. Their work includes reconstructions of the battles of Sacile and of Wagram in 1809 (now on display at the Military Academy in Vienna-Newstadt), and of the battle of Berg-Isel, which was fought in that same year.

Most unfortunately, the famous exhibits: "Custozza" and "Aspern," formerly in the Vienna Military Museum, were completely destroyed during the Second World War.

Those several exhibits, in three-dimensional settings, are more closely related to the *scale model* (as that form was defined when we considered the "Battle of Lodi") than to the true diorama with its *trompe-l'œil* effects. By that difference, their appeal is definitely heightened.

Great Britain has not lagged behind in the development of dioramas. Worth telling is the story of Captain W. Siborne, who, about 1816, was commissioned to supervise the building of a huge panorama commemorating the Battle of Waterloo. After extensive surveys made on the battlefield itself, he interviewed men who had witnessed the combat. Then he began the work, which was not completed for several years and which brought him to the verge of bankruptcy. Because the appropriation was not adequate, he had personally assumed responsibility for the major part of the cost. The diorama that he unveiled in 1838 may now be seen in

Whitehall at the Royal United Service Museum, a shrine devoted to trophies and glorious souvenirs of the three armed services—navy, cavalry and infantry, and air force. This diorama comprises not less than 180,000 figurines, which have a height of approximately 12 mm. That enormous assemblage serves rather to suggest a teeming mass than to portray soldiers in action.

Siborne then undertook a second scale model, depicting the famous charge of English cavalry in the vicinity of Haye-Sainte on the Waterloo battlefield. Here the participants were executed with much greater care than was given to those of his first endeavour. This diorama, completely rebuilt after having suffered serious damage, was assigned to the Tower of London.

One of the most famous, deservedly, of the series of dioramas in England is that given to the United Service Museum by the well-known Leipzig collector Otto Gottstein, whose significant creations in the field of tin figurines have already been mentioned.

Fleeing from Nazi persecution in 1930, Gottstein took up residence in London. There he found collaborators, and assembled enough material to set up fifteen dioramas, which had substantially identical dimensions—30 by 48 inches. They were concerned with outstanding events in British history, to wit:

Julius Caesar Approaching the English Coast (55 B.C.)
The Battle of Hastings (1066)
The Attack on Saint-Jean d'Acre (1191)
The Battle of Crécy (1346)
The Meeting on the Field of the Cloth of Gold (1520)
The Review at Tilbury by Queen Elizabeth I (1588)
The Battle of Marston Moor (1644)
The Battle of Blenheim (1704)
The Battle of Plassey (1757)
The Battle of Quebec (1759)
The Guards' Last Square at Waterloo (1815)
The Charge of the Light Brigade at Balaklava (1854)
The Battle of Ulundi (1879)
The Battle of Flers, on the Somme (1916)
D-Day: Debarkation in Normandy (1944).

It should be mentioned that, with the exception of the last named, the dioramas were peopled with figurines from nearly all of the commercial and private producers. The list of those sources is too long to itemize.

Through the courtesy of the curator of the United Service Museum, we are privileged to describe two of the units in the diorama of "The Battle of Hastings." In the first, William of Normandy is engaged in combat with the Anglo-Saxons of King Harold, and the scene depicts the decisive phase of that battle. The Anglo-Saxons, deceived by a feint of the Normans, who have simulated a rout, leave their entrenchments. Harold, who is with his brothers Gurth and Leofwin, has been struck in the eye by an arrow and mortally wounded. In the next unit we see the Norman cavalry debouching after the about face that was to bring victory. In support are the archers, who let fly a cloud of arrows on the Anglo-Saxons.

The diorama of "The D-Day Debarkation in 1944" must also be mentioned. The left wing of the British sector, to the west of the Orne River is depicted. Sherman tanks are cleaning out the nests of enemy defense. On the beach, the first attack waves have gained a foothold, while in the Channel barges protected by fighter planes are bringing in reinforcements of men and *matériel*. Bombers in the sky provide cover for the entire operation. The tableau, making manifest the close co-operation between the three service arms, is particularly appropriate for this museum, consecrated as it is to the glory of those arms. The diorama reflects the talent of M.D.C. Stokes, the eminent British specialist who was a collaborator of Otto Gottstein.

Another work by the same artist, and one also concerned with disembarkation, was presented by the British Government to the Inter-Allied Museum at Arromanches to perpetuate the memory of the heroes who gave their lives on the beaches of Normandy in 1944. Productions by Stokes, on an infinite variety of subjects, are to be found in many museums and private collections.

We are about to observe the initial use of *ronde-bosse* figurines, albeit of small size, as personages in the diorama, for which tin soldiers were hitherto used almost exclusively. As the fully formed model soldiers gained popularity, particularly in France, enthusiasts began to arrange them in small groups, on mounts in which their bases were embedded, and hence concealed. A few accessories and a simple background provided atmosphere for the scene thus contrived.

Excellent examples of such groupings—which collectors rightly hold in high esteem—are to be seen in the "Episode in the War Between the States" by the military painter Eugène Leliepvre. Northern and Southern cavalry come face to face in a composition that may well be described as daring because its maker had to reckon with the not inconsiderable weight of the horses. To the same competent hands we owe "A Scene at the Watering Trough," a tableau that like the one last mentioned, is a part of the Mathiot Collection. Here the completely independent components show all the charm that can be attained in such an ensemble, which, it must be admitted, would gain little by the addition of a background.

From that level of accomplishment to the diorama is a short step, quickly taken. *Ronde-bosse* figurines are about to come on stage. There must, however, be some modification in the scale of the setting, which henceforth must correspond to that of the figurines. That scale is reduced, approximately, from 1:55 to 1:30. The increased volume of the diorama makes it more suitable for display in a museum or exhibition than in a private collection, where the dimensions are really too large for convenience.

Here again there was public acceptance of a new concept that was much more realistic, more lifelike, and therefore more interesting.

The Navy Museum in Paris has on display a tableau, "Whale Fishing," by the painter G. Fouillé that is typical of the arrangements we consider intriguing because they are sufficient unto themselves. There are also several interesting dioramas the same artist has built around the theme of daily life on shipboard. In those colorful and sometimes humorous scenes, much of the charm is contributed by scale models of various vessels.

A recent addition to that collection is "The Return of Marines and Legionnaires from Action on the Joncs Plain," an episode in the Indo-China war of 1953. The setting, by Eugène Leliepvre, admirably recreates the lowering sky and sultry atmosphere of an uninviting landscape. For that subject, the diffused lighting, in a low key, is perfect.

In the same excellent museum were recently displayed two tableaux, also by Fouillé, that evoke a very different reaction. "The Battle of Bir-Hakeim," in the Museum of the Foreign Legion, is admired both for its setting, an arid stretch of sun-bleached desert, and for its models of tanks, which exemplify the principles of perspective already discussed. The illusion is more striking than could have been achieved by strict conformity to a three-dimensional scale. In the immediate foreground, human figures made of plaster and other materials serve to heighten the feeling of depth. The accompanying photograph (p. 73) might well have been taken on the spot, by an eyewitness to the action.

For contrast, let us examine "Soldiers of the 'Royal des Vaisseaux' Regiment in 1760," from the Gritton Collection. In a corner of the forest (perhaps at Marly, or at Versailles) Hubert-

Robert has recreated a detachment of recruits, in jackets and trousers, learning the manual of arms, while on the other bank of the stream (unfortunately not included in our illustration) the drum major drills his corps. The figurines in both of the tableaux were made by Mme. Métayer. In due course, we shall consider the dioramas on exhibit in the Figurine Museum at Compiègne.

Recognition must certainly be given to an outstanding diorama at the Gravelotte Museum entitled "France Returns the Bodies of Prussian Guard Soldiers Killed During the Battles of

BIR HAKEIM *(May 27 to June 11, 1942). Rommel, during his drive to Cairo and Suez, crashed into a strong point held by the troops of General Koenig. The legionnaires, after rejecting three successive ultimatums, destroyed a large number of enemy tanks and breached the Italo-German lines to link up with the main body of British troops. Part of a diorama by Leliepvre, with figurines by Métayer. (Museum of the Foreign Legion.)*

1870." That work, by Dr. Christ of Bonn, takes us back to June, 1893. It features an extraordinary cast of characters military and civilian, in the form of tin figurines obtained from many, many sources. Consideration being given to the large number of personages—several thousand —to the quality of their execution, and to the nicety with which they are positioned, this is perhaps the most important diorama now on display in France.

That, unfortunately, completes the roster of dioramas to be seen in French museums. There are, of course, some excellent exhibits in the hands of private collectors. But it seems regrettable that no one has taken the trouble to assemble, for the large museums and national show places visited each year by throngs of tourists, a series of dioramas commemorating the outstanding pages of French history. As far as experience with other countries goes, there is ample evidence, if it were needed, to prove that serious interest is engendered by exhibits of the kind in question when their subject matter is wisely chosen, and when their execution is entrusted to competent specialists for whom adequate means are made available.

The fact was quickly grasped by the Americans. Although they were, as we shall see, the last to join the ranks of collectors of small soldiers, they were at least the most adept in adopting a means of artistic expression having definite pedagogic worth. Whether the initiative comes from private foundations, as numerous as they are active, or from governmental departments, there is an ever increasing use of dioramas, temporary or permanent, in locations where they may be viewed by the greatest number of spectators.

For the United States, as was the case for other countries, we can cite only a few examples. The museum at West Point includes a number of exhibits devoted to military tactics. Among them are "The Battle of Crécy," with figurines made in England by John Greenwood, and "An Ambush in the Heart of an American Forest, circa 1750." Perhaps the most remarkable, which is reproduced here through the courtesy of Colonel Frederick Todd, curator of the museum, is devoted to an episode in the famous Battle of Gettysburg. The scene depicts the third day of that bloody struggle; the Confederates, after the repulse of Pickett's Charge, have

been forced to retreat. The overall effect is restrained, and impressive. The quality of the figurines, which in the foreground have a height of more than 15 cm., is admirable.

Understandably, the Civil War, abounding as it does in legendary episodes that have too often been distorted in the endless fictional accounts, affords one of the most popular themes—particularly in the states where the most significant combats were waged. In Pennsylvania, where the fraternity of collectors is large, an outstanding diorama of heroic proportions reproduces the Battle of Gettysburg, where the fate of a nation was decided.

The Atlanta Museum, on its side, has on view a most effective diorama showing the capture of the city by General Sherman, whose action in bisecting the Army of the South sounded the death knell of the Confederacy.

Another memorable period in American history was the Revolutionary War. Anderson House, headquarters of the Society of the Cincinnati in Washington, is a shrine devoted alike to the early days of the Republic and to Franco-American friendship. That society is made up of descendants of comrades of Washington, whose little known insignia they proudly display. Its French branch comprises descendants of French officers who fought under the orders of Rochambeau and Bouillé.

In addition to the priceless souvenirs that have been assembled in the exhibition rooms at Anderson House, there are groups of figurines representing, not only the French general staff, but all of the uniforms and regimental flags that were associated with the French expeditionary force.

The city of Yorktown, Virginia, on Chesapeake Bay, is known throughout the world because of the victory won there on October 19, 1781, by the small army of Washington and Rochambeau. In that "museum city", souvenirs of the siege of Yorktown are religiously preserved. Redoubts and batteries, with their bronze fieldpieces, have been reconstructed. The houses that served as headquarters for the allied command have been supplemented by a museum of military relics and dioramas. Among the latter may be cited "The Surrender," showing Major General B. Lincoln of the American forces receiving Brigadier General O'Hara, whom Cornwallis had designated to negotiate

74

for cessation of hostilities. The surrender takes place in the presence of French and American detachments, while in the distance an English column marches out of the city with flags furled.

Other tableaux are "The Washington Battery," in which George Washington, inspecting one of the siege batteries, fires a fieldpiece trained on the city; and "The Carrying of the Tenth Redoubt," a nighttime scene in which a detachment of allied infantry, swarming over the defenses, takes the British sentinels by surprise.

The city of Albany, New York, has organized an exposition in honor of the discoverers of America. Here prominence is given to a series of displays and dioramas commemorating: the discovery of the Hudson River by the navigator Verrazano (1524); Champlain discovering the lake that bears his name (1609); Hudson exploring the Hudson River (1659); and the Clinton-Sullivan Expedition (1779). Other dates of importance in the history of the New World are likewise recalled by the exposition, of which the crowning feature is a "Yorktown Surrender."

The one hundred and fiftieth anniversary of the landing of Rochambeau and his troops was similarly and effectively celebrated by the city of Newport.

In short, there is hardly an anniversary or a "convention"—and goodness knows they are not infrequent on the United States side of the Atlantic—that fails to provide incentive for expositions of the kind with which we have been concerned.

DEBARKATION PRACTICE BY A DETACHMENT OF IMPERIAL GERMAN MARINES IN THE CAMEROONS. *Circa 1910. Part of a diorama peopled with cardboard figurines designed and painted by Koekkoek. Background by Van Gisteren. (Dutch Military Museum, Leyden.)*

FAMOUS FIGURINES

If this study were limited to figurines made of tin, or fashioned from any lead alloy, it would then have to omit many creations that are of great interest from the viewpoints of history, artistic merit, and ingenious embellishment.

Wood, which was certainly one of the first materials employed by man—as is evidenced by the Egyptian soldiers shown in the opening pages of this volume—has had its devotees from the earliest days to the present time. We intentionally say nothing of wooden toys, which for centuries have been made as playthings for children, but which lie beyond the perimeter of our subject.

The unusual wood soldiers that make up some of the rare and priceless exhibits in the

SAPPER OF THE SWISS GUARDS, *1790, and* FIRST CONSUL GUIDE, *1800. Infantry uniforms. Of wood, carved by Clémence. (Figurine Museum, Compiègne.)*

Figurine Museum at Compiègne have been mentioned by many writers, but to the best of my knowledge they have not previously been illustrated. They are the handiwork of Clémence, an artisan born in Paris in 1749, who quickly acquired unusual skill in making wood carvings of the soldiers and civilians of his day. It was his daily habit to fare forth to the Tuileries Garden, where, seated on his favorite bench, he plied his jackknife to turn out little people that were sold to members of the nobility. In the words of his youngest daughter, folks of high social status "really appreciated the worth of his work."

From his hands we have a varied collection of some seventy-five pieces, including two carriages to which horses are harnessed. They were acquired from one of his sons by M. de Marsy, an enlightened collector who loaned them to the town museum at Vivenel, whence they were transferred to the Figurine Museum. There is an intriguing, six-windowed Louis XV coach, with three green-uniformed footmen and two passengers. There is a two-horse carriage, curiously slung, in which a member of the National Guard is taking his wife for a ride. There is a mounted hussar, probably of the time of Bercheny in pantaloons, blue dolman, and pelisse, and two or three other mounted horsemen. Likewise there are unmounted cavalrymen whose height, like that of the infantrymen, varies from 15 to 20 cm. Also shown are mounted grenadiers, hussars, and Louis XVI dragoons, with distinctive coloration that often permits identification. There are dragoons and light infantrymen in the uniforms of the Republic and of the Convention, as well as First Consul Guides, whose existence was somewhat ephemeral. And there are infantrymen, noncoms as well as privates, to say nothing of soldiers of the French Guard, sappers, members of the Swiss Guard and of the Irish Clare Regiment, together with the King's Constitutional Guard, the National Guard of 1789/90, artillerymen, soldiers of the Light Infantry and Line Infantry, grenadiers, and the Volunteers of '92.

AT THE HORSE RACE. *Two phases of an obstacle jump. From a series analyzing successive positions. Carved in wood by General Angenot. (Angenot Collection, Aix-en-Provence.)*

The Revolution was, at times, a period of vexation for the wood-carver, whose clientele consisted of aristocrats. He found it necessary to modify soldiers that still sported the white cockade and, alas, to destroy an entire exhibit representing the Place des Victoires, at the center of which stood the old statue of Louis XIV with nations in chains at his feet. These touching reminders of the army of Louis XVI, and of the Revolution, remain of real interest, despite the facts that their execution was at times ingenuous and awkward; that their creator—other authors to the contrary notwithstanding—did not become a celebrity or enjoy a royal clientele.

Clémence died in 1801, leaving unfinished the members of a circus troop that he had started during his last illness. Other creations of his were still extant, some fifty years ago, at Clermont, in the Oise, where he had lived with his children.

Of the same period, although of very different technique, are the two polychrome statuettes that my friend Jean Brunon has kindly permitted me to illustrate. They were made in Germany, during the French occupation, by Nicholas Fichtel of Strasbourg. On the base of the statuettes, which stand 21 cm. high, one may read: *Ano 1796, Fichtel fecit.*

The first represents a regimental line soldier clad in pantaloons and striped cotton jacket. His blue greatcoat with scarlet collar and facings is badly worn at the elbows and seams, which speaks volumes for the condition of military equipment at that time. He holds a chicken that has been "liberated." His equipment includes a canteen and a tobacco pouch, which is dangling from the handle of his tinderbox.

The second, a light infantry carabineer, wears a shako, and his uniform is in much better condition. Each sports the eccentric neck scarf, an item deliberately emphasized by the sculptor, who overlooked no single detail characteristic of these soldiers who were to make the world tremble before them.

Quite different in quality, but much closer to our times, are the statuettes of painted oak that are featured in the Military Museum at Edinburgh. Those eighty-two figurines, on foot and ahorse, display the uniforms worn by Scottish troops between 1633 and 1918. They were commissioned by the Duke of Atholl, and made under the supervision of the sculptor Pilkington Jackson, who first prepared a plaster model for each figurine. In seven great groups, they present the successive transformations in military habiliments throughout a period of three centuries. Each corps includes six or seven figurines, officers as well as privates, in fatigue, campaign and parade dress.

Their easy postures and remarkably lifelike attitudes are perfectly reproduced in the photographs, which the curator of Edinburg Castle

AN OFFICER OF THE DRAGOONS, 1810. A wood carving. Height 10 cm. (By, and from the Collection, of General Angenot, Aix-en-Provence.)

most graciously had made for the author. They speak for themselves, and make manifest the results that can be obtained when, after careful documentation, the production of models is entrusted to competent artisans.

Wood was likewise the medium selected by General P. Angenot for the extraordinary horsemen that astound even those who have little comprehension of the possibilities of historical figurines. (There are involved also some supplementary materials, to which attention will presently be given.) After making many sketches of horses in action, Angenot, a distinguished artist, sought another method of expression. What did he do? He took a piece of dry basswood and a penknife and went to work. During the ten years following his initial attempts, he modified, developed, and improved a technique that is his alone. The secret of his success? In the first place, he rode horseback every morning. He then took over a group of novice equestriaus, to whom he taught the fine points of an art

which we think of as having reached perfection. During the training of mounts and riders, and while correcting unprofessional attitudes, his mind was occupied with the miniature horse that he would create on the morrow.

One result is "The Cavalry of the First Empire", which at first glance captivates the beholder because it was made in a way utterly different from any other known today.

Being forever freed of the terrible handicap represented by the weight of a metal horse (because his weighs no more than one ounce including the rider and the base), Angenot can, when he wishes, balance his steed on the tip of one horseshoe. Thus we have the dragoon officer leading the charge of his squad, and the hussar executing a sword thrust as he stands in the stirrups.

Figurines of this quality cannot be explained or described. Scrutinize them with care; analyze the details, from the saber scabbard that dangles from its frogs to the rhythm of the galloping horse; and note that the physical effort of the rider is at one with that of his mount.

General Angenot sculptured the clearing of a steeplechase obstacle in a dozen successive jump-positions. This sequence of phases is so accurate and so true to life that it recalls the analyses of motion made by Marey with his well-known apparatus.

At the risk of invoking his wrath, I am going to reveal some of the unusual materials employed—I almost said invented—by the general. The horseman has a framework of brass or iron wire that is covered with glued-up doeskin. Pasted-up paper is used for the coat, shabrack, saddlecloth and holsters. The general has a particular fondness for cigarette paper, which when laminated with paste, produces some

A HORSEMAN OF THE TENTH HUSSARS. *1810-1812. A wood carving, by General Angenot. (Angenot Collection, Aix-en-Provence.)*

ZOUAVE AND CANTINIÈRE. *Second Empire. Of painted pipe clay. Height, 8 cm. (Collection of the author.)*

the amusement and instruction of the Dauphin" in the seventeenth century.

A fortunate chance directed my steps, in the Carnavalet Museum in Paris, to a showcase containing one of the very rare collections (dating from the eighteenth century) of ancient cardboard soldiers. That assemblage, one of the few now extant, is the property of a private collector. The work is that of Jean-Baptiste Denis Le Sueur (1748-1826), great-grandnephew of the famous artist Le Sueur and municipal administrator of the city of Paris during the Revolution. In the handwriting of Jean-Baptiste one may read, on the back of a cardboard reproduction of the royal coach, the following inscription: "King Louis XV and his Daughters Enter Paris, through the Porte St. Martin, en route from Compiengne" *(sic)*.

That magnificent coach of state, in red and gold lacquer with decorated and varnished panels, is drawn by eight horses. The driver and three footmen wear the royal livery—blue coats with scarlet facings and scarlet jackets and trousers. The seams are trimmed with crimson braid that shows a fine chain-motif in white. The coach,

A HORSEMAN OF THE ROYAL ESCORT. *Cardboard soldier. (Bibault de l'Isle Collection. Carnavalet Museum, Paris.)*

suprising results. Bookbinder's leather, skived and then thinned down, serves for all the leather parts of trappings and equipment. Epaulets are made from gold or silver embroidery thread. Sword blades, which of course may be withdrawn from their scabbards, are cut with scissors from razor blades that have been annealed and then retempered. Braidwork on the hussar's dolman is of silk passementerie.

The whole secret is in choosing, and in knowing how to utilize, the materials. Buttons are stamped from metallic paper with a die made by removing the ball fom a ball-point pen. Helmet streamers and horses' manes are of nylon floss, treated by an undisclosed process.

There is nothing more to do except to paint the horseman and his mount.

Next in popularity to wood, among construction materials employed in the early days, was cardboard, or paper pasted on cardboard, from which the subject was carefully cut, and painted. We have already cited the impressive number of cardboard soldiers that were ordered "for

◀ Above, left: NOMCOM OF THE FRENCH GUARDS. *Time of Louis XVI.* NONCOM OF THE KING'S CONSTITUTIONAL GUARD, *1791. By Clémence. Height 18 cm.;* above, right: DRAGOON OF THE NOAILLES REGIMENT, SOLDIER OF THE CLARE INFANTRY REGIMENT *and* DRAGOON OF THE COLONEL-GENERAL REGIMENT. *Circa 1790.* Below: AN OFFICER OF THE CONSTITUTIONAL GUARD TAKES HIS WIFE FOR A DRIVE. *Wood carvings by Clémence. (Figurine Museum, Compiègne.)*

which stands 11.5 cm. high, has no base: its wheels are ingeniously inserted in parallel grooves formed in the material that represents the ground, and the figurines are set up in the same manner. The background is most skillfully executed in *trompe l'œil* style.

The king, surrounded by his five daughters, is in an embroidered costume of pink silk, and is bareheaded. He wears around his neck the blue ribbon of the Order of the Holy Spirit. The lifelike escort consists of the light horse of the King's Guard and of the First and Second Companies of Musketeers, who are preceded by trumpets, kettledrums, and banners. Each of the figurines (standing 75 mm. high) is individually designed, with its own stance and expression, and some of them are truly amusing. The honors are paid by the French Guards, in blue uniforms trimmed with white braid—grenadiers, fusiliers, drummers, and standard bearers—and also by the Swiss Guard, dressed in red, with sappers, drums, and flags.

The ensemble is well conceived, full of color and life. Here again we see the difference between research that uncovers the smallest details of costumes worn in earlier days and dull descriptions that are often unreliable.

Some twelve years ago, the scholarly Paul Martin, curator of the Strasbourg Museums, published a complete and admirably illustrated volume on the subject in question, which he is particularly well qualified to discuss. With his kind permission, I have borrowed from that work some of the comments that follow.

At the outset it should be explained that cardboard soldiers may be hand drawn, cut out and painted, or they may be engraved on wood or on copper and printed on paper in groups of kindred or disparate subjects. Toward the close of the seventeenth century, rather crudely colored wood engravings of such groups of soldiers were published in Augsburg, Nuremberg, and Leipzig. Our interest, however, lies in the models that first appeared in Strasbourg.

Between 1776 and 1781 a former cavalry officer, Pierre François Isnard, made and published a series of wood engravings on French cavalry troops that has for many years provided collectors with basic information. Shortly thereafter, Striedbeck engraved his "Cavalry Conforming to the Regulations of 1786." Then, in 1791, he produced "The Infantry of the National Guard." These two service arms were known, from the respective colors of their uniforms, as the "Reds" and the "Blues," because at that time the infantry was still dressed in white.

At about the same time, famous collections were prepared by the Landgrave of Hesse-Darmstadt, who was at once a colonel of the Royal German Cavalry Regiment and of the Royal Hesse-Darmstadt Infantry. That prince ordered the court painters to duplicate in cardboard figurines both French troops and German troops. All of them, unhappily, were destroyed during the Revolution.

AN OFFICER OF THE LANCERS. *An Epinal print, before being colored. Second Empire. Height, 10 cm. (Collection of the author, Paris.)*

MASTER OF THE KING'S REGIMENT. *Circa 1680. Height, 40 cm. (By, and from the collection of, Leliepvre, Paris.)*

Throughout the long period of the wars of the Revolution and Empire, Strasbourg, as a sort of military roundhouse and warehouse, witnessed the march past of many army corps, which, before crossing the Rhine, had camped in the public squares and been billeted with the inhabitants of that city. Among the citizens who noted details of costume that were new or not previously known was the famed baker Boersch, who subsequently drew silhouettes that he cut out and painted.

Major Lévêque, a medical officer who had retired to Strasbourg before the end of the First Empire, followed the lead of Callot and devoted his leisure hours to sketching and painting the "Miseries of War," including scenes of battle, field hospitals, and associated medical services, as well as prisoners of war. As may be observed from photographs now in the Medical Museum at the Val-de-Grâce Hospital, the work of that military artist reveals many details that would otherwise be obscure.

Barthel, the printer, whose popularity endured through the Restoration, left some of our most valuable plates.

The advent of lithography gave much wider scope to military prints and permitted publishers to enlist the services of artists who were more talented than the earlier artisans. The former stiffness in attitude is not seen in lithographed views of soldiers in bivouac, on the march, on pillaging forays, or in combat. Particular credit is due to Silbermann, who, in 1845, perfected a process for printing lithographs in color. He was responsible for the well-known plates "The Imperial Guard of Napoleon III," from which soldiers were cut, colored, provided with mounting studs, and sold by the boxful. They were also furnished in sheets, printed in black and ready for coloring by collectors, whose name already was legion.

Ganier-Tanconville, the painter who lived from 1845 to 1936, is known to collectors for the many books on military history he illustrated. His work insured the survival of the cardboard soldier even as it transmitted the tradition to a new, and now contemporary, generation of military artists.

In 1931 the Strasbourg Historical Museum arranged an exposition for which the prime mover, Fritz Kieffer—a collector of high repute — assembled more than 36,000 little soldiers that had been drafted from the large private collections of Th. Carl, Paul Schmid, J. Sigel, P. Reiber, and, of course, from their dean, Jules Schneider.

Outstanding among the exhibits in that museum are "The Arrival of Louis XV at Strasbourg in 1744," with corporations in military formation against a striking background by Ganier-Tanconville; the firemen and legendary pontoniers of Strasbourg, by Georges

MAN ON A TRICYCLE. *Articulated figurine of silver. Made in Holland, about 1880. Height, 5 cm. (Collection of Mme. J. Ruby, Paris.)*

Klaenschi; and the honor guards of 1805, by Schilder.

Finally reference must be made to the Army Museum in Paris and its display of Strasbourg soldiers from the famous Würtz Collection, consecrated to the First Empire. Of the 20,000 pieces that constitute that collection, only a portion can be placed on public exhibition.

Here again are involved specialized techniques in both the painting and the delicate cutting-out operation, which is not done with scissors.

Because of their large size and the care given to their preparation, cardboard soldiers have unusual documentary value. In most instances, having been drawn from life, they show uniforms exactly as they were worn at a given period, including departures from the regulations that were supposedly then in force. Fidelity of that order is the constant preoccupation of the collector who specializes in unique pieces.

Silbermann's idea was picked up in 1900 by the Parisian firm of Hachette, which published, for young people, a "French Army" in the uniforms of that time. The soldiers were chromo-lithographed in faithful colors on stout cardboard that was die-cut and embossed, and each was provided with a mounting peg of wood. Infantrymen were 16 cm. tall, and cavalrymen were in proportion. The series included Zouaves, Algerian riflemen, spahis, African light infantry, line infantry, cuirassiers, light cavalry, the Republican Guard with bands and trumpeters, mountain light infantry, dragoons, hussars, and Paris firemen. The complete collection, which I had an opportunity to examine before the war, constitutes a magnificent military review, in which each corps displays its flag or standard.

CANNONEER. *Eighteenth century. Silver figurine. Made in Holland. Height 35 mm. (Collection of Mme. J. Ruby, Paris.)*

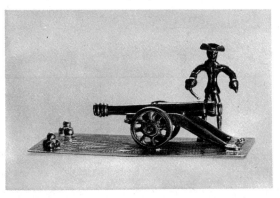

CUIRASSIER OF THE NINTH REGIMENT. *Miniature manikin. By Rousselot, who personally made the uniform and armament components, including helmet and cuirass. (Rousselot Collection, Paris.)*

Those soldiers were sold in boxes containing one, four, or twelve regiments, at prices ranging from 2.5 francs to 13.5 francs. What a glorious epoch! Today, examples of soldiers printed by Hachette are very rare indeed.

But the cardboard soldier has by no means been forgotten. Several groups of collectors skilled in design and color are carrying on the art. Among those in France may be mentioned A. Bronner, G. Cartier, M. Lairez, and M. Planchet, whose excellent work was seen at a recent exposition in Paris. Lucien Rousselot, the military painter, has created two lovely series: "The French Army in the Seventeenth Century," inspired by Delaistre's water colors, and "The Imperial Guard of the First Empire." Those groups are painted on the back as well as on the front.

A few specialists have achieved a pleasing impression of relief by pasting up in several thicknesses some parts of the soldier's uniform and equipment, including saber and sabretache. The horse's hoofs are built up in the same way. After this lamination, the soldier is given a coat of colorless varnish that serves to enhance the colors.

THE SWISS GUARD AND ITS FLAGS. *Time of Louis XV. Cardboard soldiers. Height, 75 mm. Accompanied by the French Guards, they pay homage to the King. (Carnavalet Museum, Paris.)*

This "Review of the Cardboard Soldiers" would not be complete if it overlooked the very important collection of the works of the Dutch military painter H. W. Koekkoek, at the military Museum in Leyden. That artist, who lived for twenty years in London (which he left in 1923), was an accomplished military portraitist; as a hobby, he cut out and painted, between 1900 and 1910, hundreds of figurines representing the armies of different countries,

with particular emphasis on German colonial troops.

Some of his figurines are included in two dioramas that are among the outstanding exhibits of the Leyden Museum. One of them depicts, against a background painted by Van Gisteren, a sham battle among the Cameroon auxiliary troops ("Schutztruppe Kamerun"). The other reproduces a disembarkation drill by a detachment of German marines in Africa.

Koekkoek found a disciple in the person of the Dutch painter Bottema, who designed the figurines for the diorama "The Battle of Mook" (1574). In that exhibit the pikemen, musketeers, drummers, and standard-bearers have a height of 9 cm., helmets included. They exemplify a method of mounting that I believe had been used only by Bottema. The drawings were pasted on a thin sheet of aluminum, which, in turn, was glued to Bristol board before the piece was cut out. The painting was done by M. C. Boode, a colorist whose work is very popular among Dutch collectors. The mounting technique imparts perfect rigidity to the soldiers and their accessory equipment, and totally eliminates any necessity for reinforcements, which are always more or less visible and unesthetic.

M. A. C. Paardekooper, director of the Leger Museum, has very kindly loaned the several original figures that are reproduced here.

The renown of the Strasbourg soldier had hardly spread beyond the borders of the eastern provinces of France, since at that time communications were rather generally limited to neighborly relations.

But then, along came Jean-Charles Pellerin of Epinal, a maker of playing cards and colored pictures, who had been the publisher of "The Saints"—the wood engravings on religious subjects that once were pinned or pasted to the walls and cupborad doors of the humblest farmhouses. During the Revolutionary period, his modest business was on its last legs. Having some knowledge of Strasbourg soldiers, he essayed the new medium by making, with his own hands, wood engravings that plagiarized the work of Barthel. During the Restoration, he enlisted the services of Réveillé, a veteran of the Napoleonic Wars who had taken part in the retreat from Russia. Pellerin taught the rudiments of the art to the old soldier.

His successor, Nicolas Pellerin, joined forces with his brother-in-law, Vadet, who had been an officer in the light cavalry. Together they modernized the production technique by making lead plates from the original woodcuts, and by updating earlier plates, replacing fleurs-de-lis with eagles on the flags, at the same time eliminating bearskin caps and substituting white cockades for those which had glorified the tricolor.

By 1830, the tricolor was again in vogue, and the Napoleonic legend was taking shape. Vadet unwittingly became a disseminator of the new thinking as he made engravings of great battles that were fought during the First Empire. His inspiration was admittedly derived, albeit with much amplification, from the battle scenes King Louis-Philippe was then having painted for Versailles. The captions on Vadet's vivid color plates bear spirited witness to the glory of the Empire.

SCOTCH SOLDIERS. *Of molded paper pulp. Painted. Accessories of metal, bases of wood. Height 9 cm. (Philippot collection, Paris.)*

BRIGADIER OF THE ELITE COMPANY OF THE FIRST HUSSARS. *First Empire. Of porcelain. Decorated in Dresden fashion. Belt and straps of leather, sword of cast metal. Height 24 cm. (By, and from the collection of, Van Gerdinge Avignon.)*

The French army, completely reorganized, won fame in Algeria, where the African army was created. The common soldier, who was then called to the colors for a seven-year stretch, had no photograph to send to the folks at home. So he sent a "regimental souvenir" that showed the brilliant colors of his uniform.

The Epinal color pictures benefited from an extraordinary method of distribution—peddling. Every year more than two thousand peddlers travelled to the east to stock up. Then, pack on back, they tramped the roads of France, hawking their low-priced wares in the smallest hamlets. For the future Napoleon III, such pictures were to prove the most effective of propaganda. To them he was to owe his overwhelming victory in the referendum through which he was named emperor.

The advent of lithography made it possible for Pinot, a meticulous draftsman, to prepare color plates of contemporaneous military achievements —the campaigns in Italy, the Crimea, China, Mexico, and, later, the Transvaal.

Indirectly, the manufacture of the Epinal color pictures (of which there were now, even in Paris, numerous imitators) contributed to a revival of interest, on the part of young people, in military costumes. This production immediately preceded the work of such famous painters as Adam, Meissonier, and Detaille. Although derived from the simplest of toys, like the tin soldier, color pictures evolved into representations that combined discernment with constantly improving quality. For that reason they are now eagerly sought by serious collectors.

Many fanciful tales have been told concerning the important series of figurines of the French Army under the Second Empire, as executed during that epoch by Frémiet, the celebrated sculptor. In an endeavour to dispel some of those myths we shall, in the quest of truth, make use of Frémiet's own words.

At the outset, let it be said that those statuettes were not ordered for the Imperial Prince, who was born in 1856. Frémiet says: "At a military review that was probably held in 1854, I was struck by the original stance of a mounted sentinel of artillery. I made a statuette of him, and the Superintendent [Monsieur de Nieuwerkerke, the Beaux-Arts superintendent, who was also a sculptor] saw it in my studio and took it to the Emperor. His Majesty suggested that the entire French Army be reproduced in the same style, and that the statuettes then be painted in colors. My acceptance was conditioned upon the right, which was granted, to offer those statuettes for sale."

They were not made of terra cotta, nor were they lead castings, despite assertions in which the name of the founder is cited. In point of simple fact, they were plaster of Paris, as their creator will confirm. Let us again call upon him to speak.

"I wondered how I could best handle the miserable business [it is a sculptor who is talking] of painting the figurines. First, I took wool flock of the kind used in coating "velvet" wallpaper. With a suitable mordant, I dyed the wool flock in the colors required for the uniforms of the little soldiers. Fur caps and sheepskin shabracks were made from chopped silk floss. Harness straps were cut from glove leather. All articles of metal—shields, weapons, helmets, and buttons —were fashioned, with microscopic care, from brass. Buttons worn by members of the Guard bore the imperial arms. The piping on pantaloons was simulated with silk sewing-thread, glued to the fabric. The collection thus executed was at least of real value for future documentation. It consisted of seventy-five different military costumes: infantry, cavalry, sutlers, drum majors, Sisters of Charity [who then served as nurses]—and of one field piece drawn by four horses..."

"At another time, Monsieur de Nieuwerkerke asked me to make a statuette of the Emperor, who, as he came from Mass at the Tuileries, was kind enough to pose for fifteen minutes. But the Empress considered his legs to be too short above the knees, so I had the privilege of beginning again!"

The priceless documentation represented by that assemblage of Second Empire troops was completely destroyed in 1871, under the Commune, by the conflagration at the Tuileries. Fortunately the sculptor, in accordance with the authority granted to him, had arranged for production by Barbedienne of some fifteen bronze models. Their ultimate disposition is unknown, but one story is that, after the collapse of the Empire, some of them were given by the Empress Eugénie to her faithful friends. Today they are exceedingly rare, and it is thanks to the inexhaustible collections of R. and J. Brunon, of Marseilles, that we are able here to show a series of those figurines that are almost unkown, even to specialists.

Pieces issued by Frémiet included the Emperor, the line carabineer, and the cuirassier, all of which were mounted. There were also the grenadier, the Zouave, the artilleryman, and the *voltigeur* of the Guard (the last named in a greatcoat); the sapper, the horse guards of Napoleon III; and, on foot, the departmental gendarme. Finally, the roster included an artillery officer of the Guard, a mounted light cavalryman, and a mounted hussar.

Of those pieces, the first eight are included in the Brunon collections.

The National Porcelain Factory at Sèvres, established at Vincennes in 1738 and moved to Sèvres in 1756, is known throughout the world for its natural and artificial porcelain and its unglazed biscuit. The Sèvres Museum of Ceramics has on display the only figurines ever turned out by that factory—a group of World War I soldiers, including poilus at a listening post, on the way back from the trenches, and in cantonment. These figurines which are 23 cm. tall, were sculptured by Paul Ducuing. An American soldier of 1917 wearing a greatcoat, a British soldier of the same period, and a second American, of 1918, with jacket and helmet, are the work of the same sculptor, who made them 28 cm. high.

Finally, from the hands of Max Blondat there is a young and intriguing soldier on leave, who is wearing a fanciful tunic and forage cap. Those poilus of porcelain inevitably bring to mind the spirited wartime sketches of Bernard Naudin. They also invite comparison with the equally rare figurines modeled by Frémiet during the Second Empire.

In the eighteenth century, figurines were also made of Dresden china, by production methods whose secrets became known in France during the second half of that century. Those concerned with military subjects of that period are deservedly in demand by collectors. It is worthy of note that a French porcelain manufacturer has recently taken up the old technique of decorated natural porcelain to produce a number of figurines in First Empire uniforms that reflect the studious documentation of L. Rousselot.

These statuettes, standing about 24 cm. high, are splendidly decorated, despite the risks to which colors are exposed in kiln-firing. Belts and straps are of fine glove leather. Rifles, sabers, and other weapons are made either of brass or of painted lead castings. In addition to an excellent brigadier of the Elite Company of the First Hussars, there are a member of the Sixth Hussars, a foot grenadier of the Guards, and a lancer of the Second Regiment of Light Horse. They are well-executed examples that reinstate an almost forgotten genre.

Deserving of consideration in this study of famous figurines are two figurines that have formed a part of the Philippot Collection in Paris since 1938. They are almost certainly the only extant specimens of a series of 140 figurines that were made for King Frederick William III, and which were formerly exhibited in the Hohenzollern Museum in Berlin. Nearly all of them were destroyed by bombardments during, World War II.

They are cast in Britannia metal and screwed to iron bases, and they are approximately 25 cm. tall. Modeling and engraving are most skillfully executed in every detail. The painting, oven-baked, is delicate and very well preserved. The first represents a grenadier of the Company of Warrant Officers of the Prussian Guard, in 1829. His mitred headgear bears a gilded plaque. The second, a grenadier of the First Regiment of Guard Infantry, is in full-dress uniform, with white plumed shako.

On their bases one looks in vain for a signature or other indication of origin. According to Hampe (*Der Zinnsoldat*, Berlin, 1924), they closely resemble work turned out between 1830 and 1840 by Du Bois, of Hanover. It seems probable, however, that they came from the studio that G. Sölke set up in Berlin in 1819.

Toward the middle of the nineteenth century, German and French manufacturers almost simultaneously began to turn out soldiers of various sizes that were molded from a paper pulp, to which they added a binder and a certain amount of plaster of Paris. That pulp-paste was incorrectly called papier mâché.

The results were definitely more popular in France than on the other side of the Rhine. Some of them could only be described as toys, as, for example, a trumpeter of the Second Horse Guards whose rectangular base of painted wood is fitted with four small lead wheels, to form the classical pulltoy. Nevertheless, it is, as are the others, quite carefully made. The horse, about 14 cm. high, has a good silhouette. His rider's uniform and the characteristic trappings are correct in form and color. The fact that the helmet has no horsetail clearly established the date as 1854. It is worthy of note that the accessories—trumpet, spurs, stirrups, and bit—are tin castings; that bridle reins and belts are of fine glove leather.

Such horsemen were sold in boxes containing six or eight, including one officer. The common soldiers were identical.

Some of the paper-pulp subjects were destined for a less easily defined market. A case in point is an officer of the Eighth Hussars, who is taller by 4 cm. and much more elegant, than the figurine just described. His rearing horse is supported by a tree trunk—a device both conventional and classic. It is admitted, once and for all, that there is nothing unwonted about the trunk of a tree beneath the belly of a horse! Even so, the steed's bearing is worthy of Carle Vernet, and of the epoch represented. His rider, wasp-waisted as becomes an officer of the light cavalry, conforms to 1954 regulations, including the high shako with drooping cock feathers. Here again the metal accessories are cast in tin and the leathers are cut from glove material. The painting is delicate, dexterous, and carefully done.

By chance I discovered in Austria an Emperor surrounded by his general staff—twelve figurines of paper-pulp, having a height of 13.5 cm. Each was mounted on an unfinished pine base, in the best Black Forest tradition. The group was packed in its original wood box, whose sliding cover bore the label "Franz-Josef et son Etat-Major". For those times, the use of French was to be expected.

The young emperor, who was then twenty-seven or twenty-eight years old, wears the uniform of a marshal—a white tunic with scarlet collar and facings; scarlet trousers with two gold stripes, and a bicorn hat with drooping plumes. He wears about his neck the Order of Marie-Thérèse, as well as decorations of other orders. There is remarkable resemblance to a portrait of him that was engraved in 1857. At his right stands the old Field Marshal Radetzky, the faithful aide-de-camp under whom he received his baptism of fire in Lombardy. The Marshal also wears the Order of the Golden Fleece, as well as the cordon of the Iron Crown. On his left, Colonel General Pejácsevics of the Hungarian Hussars is identified by the bandage over his right eye. Also recognizable are Archdukes Ferdinand and Charles-Louis.

Once again, spurs and sabers are of tin, belts and sashes are of embossed gold paper, and saber straps are of fine leather. The variety of attitudes and diversity of uniforms and headdress make it evident that each figurine was individually sculptured.

A very similar group, "Napoleon III and His Marshals," comprising thirteen statuettes of the same size and material, was shown at the exposition entitled "Marshals of France" that was held in 1922 at the Palace of the Legion of Honor. Every member of the entourage was readily identifiable, but the series, from a celebrated German collection, has now been dispersed. The identical treatment of the two groups clearly points to a common origin, which unfortunately remains unknown.

Boxes of soldiers, also molded from paperpulp and mounted on wood bases, were offered commercially. One of the most popular brought the armies of the Crimean War face to face. With a height of 9 cm., those little soldiers, although not intended for connoisseurs, like the Scotch troops here illustrated, were well made and very well painted. Their faces, colored with particular care, have the appearance of porcelain. Noteworthy is the strange, cubical box—included probably for its Scotch effect—that is used as a drum.

There are English troops, and French troops in iron-gray coats, with red trousers and the red caps that then represented the latest vogue in military headgear. There are Turks, with black eyes and palikar mustaches, wearing red chéchias. And, of course, there are Russians.

The rifles and sabers are of cast tin. The flags of all nations are of painted fabric—and,

strange to relate, they are accurate. The uniforms, too, are beyond criticism. Unfortunately, the number of "survivors," eagerly sought by collectors, is small indeed.

At a much later date, about 1890 to 1900 and for too many years thereafter, toy stores offered horrible Zouaves and infantrymen that were crudely molded, poorly painted, and ill calculated to improve the taste of the children for whom they were designed. They were very fragile. Their life-span, luckily, was brief, because they did not endure when used as tenpins!

Much more amusing are the pipe-clay figurines, about 8 cm. tall, that could be purchased for a few pennies in the tobacco shops that sold clay pipes. They date back to the

Soldiers cut from sheet iron, and painted. Articulated. The subjects are caused to "march" by a set of rods connected to toothed wheels of a diameter slightly greater than the thickness of the wood base. Second Empire. Height 4 cm. (Marchal Collection, Paris.)

Second Empire. In execution they resemble the Provençal *santons*[1] from which they were derived. (It happens, I believe, that the manufacture of clay pipes was largely confined to the south of France.) Although, as the product of two-part molds, they are unavoidably stiff in attitude, the fact that they are made of clay means that the modeling is faithfully reproduced. Among them are *cantinières*, who were then in high favor, Zouaves, infantrymen, and a few other subjects.

Along with the clay pipe, these specimens of a bygone craft have disappeared—except as they may be seen in the show windows of antique shops.

[1] *Santons* (little saints) are tiny painted figurines of terra cotta, originally developed in Provence for use in crèches, at Christmastime. They are now produced in quantity, for sale to tourists.

LOUISIANA TIGER ZOUAVE. *Civil War. Ronde-bosse figurine by Imrie. (Blum collection, New York.)*

In those same windows one may occasionally have the luck to find figurines made of silver. Those tiny pieces, standing from 3.5 to 4 cm. high, are usually of Dutch origin. They may represent soldiers of the seventeenth century, in jerkins and three-cornered hats, like the artilleryman firing his fieldpiece, or an amusing patrol preceded by a drummer thumping a drum nearly as tall as he is. There may also be small tradesmen—the fish-peddler whose pushcart is laden with fried fish; the scissors-grinder whose arms and legs, as well as a foot pedal, are articulated; and a few animated little people, like the athletic individual on the tricycle who goes into action at the push of a finger.

The Second Empire, positively prolific in unexpected inventions, has left us groups of soldiers in silhouette that, surprisingly, are cut from sheet iron and painted. Thus the Marchal Collection, in Paris, includes an imperial barge having a length of some 65 cm. In the stern, under a canopy, stands the Emperor, surrounded by several of his officers. The sailors are at their oars. The boat rests on a base formed by two parallel wood strips between which are toothed wheels of a diameter slightly exceeding the thickness of the base. When the exhibit is pushed, the sailors come to life, and thanks to a system of articulated rods, they bend to their oars and row.

The detachment of light infantry, in 1860 uniforms, with képis and baggy red pantaloons as shown in our illustration, operates on a similar principle, but here it is the legs that move in cadence when the ensemble is pushed. On the reverse side, the figurines are painted to represent *chasseurs à pied*, with blue képis, short jackets of navy blue, and trousers of horizon blue with pale yellow trimmings. For them, the speed of action may be accelerated to simulate the faster cadence characteristic of that crack outfit. Despite its age, the mechanism, although it creaks slightly, still operates in very satisfactory fashion.

... the studio, crammed with headgear, sabers and metal gear, is a cross between a museum and an old curiosity shop. Small manikins, under glass, reproduce to the most minute detail the pomp of the Prussian uniform. There stands the General, in the uniform of the Kœnigsberg Cuirassiers, listening respectfully to the orders of a splendid Manteuffel who towers ten inches

high. The uniform of the victor of Borny is complete, from the half-inch field glasses made by a Dresden optician to the General Staff satchel containing, in photographic facsimiles reduced to scale, the very dispatches that were exchanged with Steinmetz and Moltke. Could one calculate how many fir trees were felled to pay for these costly fantasies?..

(PIERRE BENOIT: *Axelle.*)

The reader will have recognized General de Reichendorff, whose curious silhouette we observed in an earlier chapter.

The novelist has made it almost unnecessary for us to comment on the small manikins because his description so vividly suggests the other, the most perfect, form of figurine.

A few words, however, must be added. Two military painters, Eugene Leliepvre and Lucien Rousselot, were the respective creators of the two figurines to which our attention is now turned. The first, an officer under Louis XIII, mounted on his steed, has a height of approximately 40 cm. Over his cloth uniform he wears a complete of suit armor—breastplate and backplate, with shoulder guards, brassarts, and elbow guards, as well as cuissards lined with buffalow hide, which descend to the knee plate. His boots, of soft leather, have the wooden heels characteristic of the period, and his burgonet helmet, with ear- and neckshields and with adjustable nosepiece, is adorned with plumes. He is armed with a great sword of Italian pattern, with straight crossguards and ivory tang. The saddle and holsters are richly ornamented with stitching, embroidery, and fringe, and in the holsters are the long-barreled pistols of that day. About his neck the officer wears the blue ribbon of the Order of the Holy Spirit (its cross, in perfect scale, is 7 mm. high), and across his breast is the white cordon of command.

For the magnificent pieces of articulated, blued-steel armor, riveted and ornamented with hammered copper, as well as for the helmet and sword, credit must be given to M. Rocheron, who is a specialist without rival in the making of small-scale arms, armor and headgear.

Leliepvre is also responsible for the "Master of the King's Regiment," of the 1680 period. That officer wears a jerkin with split skirt and sleeves of soft leather, and a cuirass of black iron. He is armed with a great sword, two small pistols whose holsters are decorated with the gold braid of his regiment, and a heavy musket. His jack boots, with flaring tops as worn in the reign of Louis XIV, have spurs of black iron and his broad felt hat has a crown of steel. His greatcoat is rolled up on the saddletree.

Lucien Rousselot, working on the same scale, has recreated for us in his "Cuirassier of the First Empire" one of the horsemen whose uniforms, equipment and arms were so meticulously shown in the color plates that were discussed in the chapter on documentation. That the figurine is a member of the Ninth Regiment is shown not only by the regimental number on the saddle bag, but also by the light yellow color of the collar, facings, and cuffs of the blue jacket, as well as by the white coat, the trousers of bleached leather, and the knee boots.

The spherical helmet, of iron with copper decorations, is topped by a crest of black horsehair and a red plume. The riveted breastplate and backplate, the copper shoulder guards and the helmet, were hand-hammered by the artist himself. Fraises of red fabric with white borders appear at neckband and armholes. The epaulets are of red wool. Trappings include horsecloth, saddlebag and chaperons of blue cloth trimmed with white wool braid, with a grenade of the same color at one corner of the horsecloth. The greatcoat, lined with that same blue, is folded, in accordance with regulations, across the cantle. In addition to cuirass and helmet, the officer is armed with a saber with iron scabbard and copper sword guard, and with a pair of pistols.

The impression produced by these manikins is the more surprising when one stops to analyze each of the component parts. It is astounding to realize that the garments, made exactly to scale, are removable, not sewn onto the figurines. Trousers, jackets, and coats, are all cut and fitted to measure, precisely as though the work were done by a tailor.

In Rousselot's studio there is a "military uniform depot" with sets of boots as worn by all service arms of all periods. The footgear is made from skived leather, with hand-tooled wrinkles. There are hats of all styles, and helmets with chin straps whose overlapping scales, cut one at a time from thin copper, are sewn on leather. There is armor that has been hammered to shape by the craftsman. The buttons, stamped out by hand, are provided with stems before they are sewn to the uniform and slipped through their buttonholes. One can imagine the labor involved in placing correctly the eighty buttons that belong on the dolman of a hussar! The blades of sabers and swords can of course be withdrawn from their scabbards, which are complete with wrist straps, rings, and appropriate fittings. Ramrods may be thrust down the muzzles of rifles and muskets of all models, which, as here displayed, are tiny masterpieces of the gunsmith's art. I spare the reader the details of saddles, bits, bridles, harnesses and their trappings, of which every single part is individually executed.

It need scarcely be added that accomplishments of this order are rare indeed. I could name not more than ten others of comparable quality—for which the price, however high, is less than proportionate to the consummate art and science involved in the perfection of such true museum pieces.

A corner devoted to EQUIPMENT STORES *for miniature manikins in the studio of L. Rousselot, the military painter. Costume components, cut and sewn by their creator, hang above pairs of boots, felt hats, and shakos of various periods. Helmets for dragoons, cuirassiers, and carabiners await their owners. Arms are aligned on the gunrack. (Rousselot Collection, Paris.)*

ARTILLERY, AND MILITARY VEHICLES

Makers of figurines did not overlook field-pieces, artillery-park equipment, or the possibilities of military and civilian vehicles. But it must be admitted that flat castings, despite the care lavished upon them by designers and mold-makers, are sadly lacking in third-dimensional effect; that the collector has difficulty in reconciling himself to the absence of volume in *matériel* that bulks large in the original.

True it is that Gribeauvals[1] of different calibers, from the largest down to mortars, with their forecarriages, and artillery-park equipment—caissons, traveling forges, pontonier wagons, ambulances of various models, and even sutler's carts—were expertly executed by Mignot, in Paris. The horses harnessed thereto are shown at rest, on the march, and in combat. The details are perfect, but—the rigs do not look as though they could roll.

[1] An eighteenth-century four-wheeled fieldpiece having a range of 1000 to 1500 yards.

ENGLISH FIELDPIECE—A NINE POUNDER. *The gun used by the British artillery during the Napoleonic Wars. By Rose Models, of London.*

That shortcoming has prompted the most fervent collectors of tin figurines to attempt a combination of horses in-the-flat with vehicles having real wheels or with fieldpieces having real gun barrels. Such endeavours, by specialists well known for their dexterity, have often been crowned with success.

Little time was to elapse before some manufacturers of *ronde-bosse* figurines—e.g., Lucotte and C.B.G. in France—began to turn out cannon of various models with horses hitched to the forecarriage, and other vehicles as well. The results, when considered as toys of quality, were excellent. The amateur collector (for whom, be it noted, those pieces were not originally intended) could complain that in silhouette and in characteristics the fieldpieces were but relative approximations; that wheels, available only in a very few models, were used indiscriminately on fieldpieces, caissons, and other vehicles. There was a small pair of wheels for the forecarriage; a large pair for the gun.

Several manufacturers of *demi-ronde-bosse* models (which were of half the standard size) found it advantageous to produce fieldpieces

having a forecarriage that defied all attempts at identification. They used the same gun barrel for English, French, and German cannon. Its color varied with the nationality, and the uniforms of the gun crew completed the illusion.

But the influence of the special-model figurine was soon to be felt.

In France, the innovator, once again, was Alexandre Ballada, who showed the way to a host of followers. At the outset, he created for the Keller Collection the charming series of horse-drawn civilian carriages that were the hit of a Champs Elysées exposition that included a wide range of equipages of the 1900 period. Among them was the mail coach shown in our illustration.

Frequently the wheel problem was solved by the use of disks of transparent plastic material that were skillfully painted to suggest motion. The horses, as we have said, were still flat.

But Ballada had higher ambitions. Working from books and diagrams on military construction, he undertook to make models of Louis XV artillery, and then of Gribeauval pieces as employed under Louis XVI and throughout the wars of the Revolution and the Empire.

Since the gun carriages of that time were made of wood, he fashioned wooden brackets

GRIBEAUVAL FOUR-CALIBER FIELD PIECE. *Gun barre of bronze, engraved with the royal cipher (Period of Louis XVI). This production model has wheels and gun carriage, not of wood but of cast metal. This is the field-piece designed to accompany infantry battalions. Model by Ballada. (Mathiot Collection, Chantilly.)*

GRIBEAUVAL CANNON. *First Empire model. With fore-carriage, munition chest, bucket, and ramrod. Model by Ballada. (Mathiot Collection, Chantilly.)*

TWELVE-CALIBER FIELDPIECE. *An exact reproduction of the model described by Surizey (1745). The gun barrel, cast in bronze and turned and bored, is delicately chased, and bears the royal arms. The heavy wood carriage, and the wheels banded with iron, are painted red. The gun stands between three powder kegs and a munitions cart of the Vigny pattern. Model by Ballada. (Mathiot Collection, Chantilly.)*

and transoms, which were assembled in accordance with the desired scale. In similar fashion, wheels were built up from wood spokes and rims. Tires and fittings of metal were then added. Gun barrels were cast in bronze, lathe-turned, and reamed to the desired caliber. Then they went to the engraver, who after decorating them with the arms of France or of the Prince de Bourbon, Grand Master of Artillery, added such inscriptions as were then in use.

Thus were produced the splendid models of 16-, 12- and 8-caliber cannon that are now in the Mathiot Collection, and of which very few copies exist. They are supplemented by munition carts with kegs of powder, a gun

derrick with its system of pulleys, and a two-wheeled cart for the transport of the copper pontoons used in bridge-building.

The last of the plates engraved to illustrate General Gribeauval's "Construction Tables for Major Pieces of Artillery Equipment" were not completed until the eve of the Revolution. When that work can be consulted (the edition was very small), one need not look further for essential data on gun carriages, forecarriages, caissons and gun barrels.

With confidence gained from his experience in constructing *matériel* used in the days of the Regency and Louis XV, and recognizing the long interval during which, with many modifications, Gribeauval designs were to be followed, Alexandre Ballada undertook to duplicate for artillery his eminently successful accomplishments with cavalry.

Beginning with the several components of a gun carriage—brackets, transoms, axles and wheels—he made separate molds of bronze, so that a hard alloy could be used for the castings. Those parts could then be assembled by soldering. Gun barrels of different calibers, cast in bronze or copper, were lathe-turned, bored, and fitted with suspension lugs. The result was a four-caliber fieldpiece of the model assigned to the infantry in the ratio of two guns per battalion. That piece was used throughout all of the campaigns of the Revolution and the Directoire. Then came the carriage of the 12-caliber campaign gun (later known as the "System of the Year XII," which was perfected in 1803.

The 4-caliber was replaced by a 6, the old 8-caliber by a 12. The new carriage could be considered as standard, because when the trunnions were fitted with sleeves, it could accomodate barrels of various calibers. It is most unfortunate that only a very few of the models thus produced were available to collectors.

Nothing of equal quality has since been made in France. Devotees of special models have perforce undertaken, at their own expense and in accordance with the documentation mentioned above, the construction of artillery pieces made in part of wood and in part of metal. While the results in general have been laudable, the attendant difficulties go far to explain why even the more important private collections are decidedly poor in cannon.

It therefore seems appropriate to commend such foreign manufacturers as W. Imrie in the United States and, more recently, Russell Gammage of London, for having produced properly designed cannon. Particularly good is the English nine-pounder, of the time of the Napoleonic Wars. The military *matériel* created by Britain's, also of London, is well known and widely admired. It is mentioned here solely for the record, because its genre seems much closer to the category of miniature models—whether made of metal or of plastic—than to the world of figurines.

Bridge-building matériel of the time of Louis XV, with light pontoon cart and wood-ribbed pontoon of copper. Model by Ballada. (Mathiot Collection, Chantilly.)

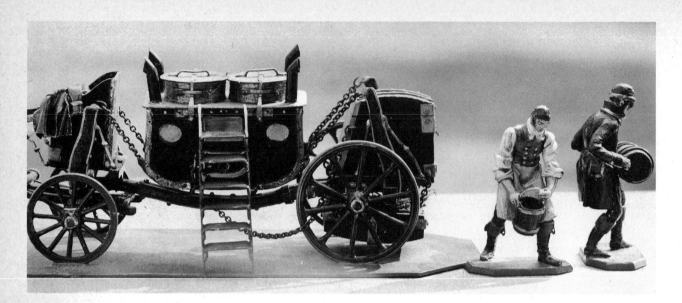

THE EMPEROR'S FIELD KITCHEN. *By Leliepvre. (Mathiot Collection, Chantilly.)*

But let us leave the *ultima ratio regum* and its destructive warriors for more pleasant and peaceful subjects.

The Mathiot Collection includes, among other marvels, a series of civilian carriages, among which it was exceedingly difficult to make a choice of what to show here.

In preference to the Emperor's covered campaign carriage—so often reproduced, even in the flat—I show the "Fliguette," a Dutch tilbury of the eighteenth century. A distinguishing feature of this graceful vehicle is that,

in the winter, it may be transformed into a sleigh. The studded harnesses are characteristic of that type of rig.

Of the same period, about 1750, is the "Désobligeante" [1]—well named because it accommodates only two passengers, who, at best, are crowded. But because it was designed for speed, and well suspended, the carriage was admirably

[1] *Désobligeante:* disobliging, unpleasant, or disagreeable.

MAIL COACH DRAWN BY SIX HORSES. *A combination of flat tin subjects with a vehicle that is built "to roll." Model by Ballada. (Keller Collection, Paris.)*

suited for the hurried aristocrat who had to travel posthaste.

"Napoleon's Campaign Kitchen," the ancestor of modern field kitchens, includes copper kettles, as well as a cook stove. Beside it, bustling about their work, are the footmen of the Emperor's household in their green campaign livery. The ensemble is the creation of the artist Eugène Leliepvre, who, to the best of my knowledge, is the only vehicle specialist in France. To his credit there are many other models, including "The Chariot of Ramses II," "The Sun King's Leather Bellows" (which Louis XIV drove himself); "The Sleigh of Catherine the Great" (based on contemporaneous documents) and "The Wiski[1] of Marie Antoinette," after Le Brun.

Everyone of them is a meticulous reconstruction, not only of the carriage, but of the harness, which is by no means the easiest part of the task.

[1] A light, high, two-wheeled cabriolet drawn by one horse.

THE CARRIAGE OF MADAME DE STAEL. *A miniature model. Horses and passengers are flat, of classical size. Only the carriage, ingeniously contrived (on the same scale) is three-dimensional. By Ballada. (Keller Collection, Paris.)*

THE AGE OF PLASTICS

After the Bronze Age and the Iron Age, we have, for better or for worse, the Age of Plastics.

The possibilities of the new age were astonishing to a Europe that had been isolated for four years. They have expanded before our eyes, not from year to year but from month to month.

Yet the origin of plastics is much older than one might suppose. Celluloid was first produced in 1870, Bakelite in 1907. Galalith[1] is even older. They were originally developed as substitutes for the more expensive raw materials

[1] A plastic made from casein.

OFFCIERS AND SOLDIERS OF THE FRENCH GUARDS. *Time of Louis XIV. Flat, plastic figurines, decorated on both sides. Height, 40 mm. After original designs by Rousselot. (Mathiot Collection, Chantilly.)*

NAPOLEON I. *Ronde-bosse plastic figurine of normal size. Weighted. By Leliepvre. (Mathiot Collection, Chantilly.)*

that they replaced, and whose essential properties they approximated. Petrochemistry, from which more than 80 per cent of today's plastics are derived, has given us new materials with properties that are unique. Their manufacture, as is well known, has necessitated a major financial investment, and their practical application, in turn, depends upon large-scale production and international distribution.

The first figurines of plastic were therefore developed for a trade of maximum potential, the toy market. Plastics were also ideal for advertising novelties because, while the cost of production equipment was high, the tremendous output was reflected in very low prices.

Preparation of the master models was wisely assigned to competent artists whose talents gave value to articles that carried extremely low price tags. Military painters like P.-A. Leroux and L. Rousselot were responsible for "A Series of Generals," "Soldiers of the First and Second Empires," "The War of 1914-1918," and even for a most attractive set of chessmen of a medieval design.

Neophyte collectors—and some who were advanced—were impressed by figurines that were easy to buy, and which invited experimentation. Several well-organized competitive exhibitions gave standing to the new figurines, which, it must be admitted, were regarded with the same ironic condescension that had been accorded to the first *ronde-bosse* pieces.

About 1952, a Parisian firm S.E.G.O.M. developed plastic figurines of a normal *ronde-bosse* format that were specifically intended for collectors. Those figurines, designed by L. Rousselot, were offered in a variety of separate pieces to which different attitudes and positions could be given. Little by little the technique progressed to a point at which ingenious amateurs achieved most creditable results. Ample evidence of the possibilities is given by "The Riding Master of Saumur."

In respect of painting, the specialists were soon divided into two schools. On the one hand, some would use only pigments specially formulated for use on plastic. Those colors, in my opinion, afford a palette that is rather limited, particularly as regards the mixture of tints. Others preferred, after application of a priming coat, to employ classical oil paints—with results that justified their choice.

In due course there came group after group of horsemen, armed from head to foot—as, for example, the soldiers of the English Guard. Such figurines were made in various size scales.

What may we now expect to see, in the realm of plastic figurines? There will certainly be surprises, if one may judge by the work now in progress at the studios of Rousselot and Leliepvre. The former has just completed "The French Army of the Seventeenth Century," with French and Swiss Guards followed by the Imperial Army. Behind the Emperor, who is on horseback and surrounded by a colorful

ROYAL NETHERLANDS GUARD. *Plastic figurines, decorated. Height, 8 cm. (Philippot Collection, Paris.)*

All of these figurines—in two sizes, 30 mm. and 55 mm.—are to be made in flat plastic, from which they will be cut out. Thanks to a new method of direct printing, they will be finished in color, on both sides.

Leliepvre has completed prototypes, *ronde-bosse* and of classical dimensions, for "The Emperor and his General Staff," a group that includes Murat, Bessières, Ney, an ordnance officer, and Roustan, the Mameluke, all of whom are on horseback. The Emperor and his mount are assembled from twenty-eight different pieces, a technique permitting variations in the position of the horse (for which different legs are available) and his trappings. The parade horsecloth, for example, may be replaced by the horsecloth used in the field.

For the first time, the horsemen are weighted. That improvement silences complaints directed at the annoying lightness usually associated with figurines made of plastic.

RIDING MASTER OF SAUMUR. *Ronde-bosse plastic figurine, with "SEGOM" mounting. (Biéville Collection, Paris.)*

general staff, are seen the principal corps of the Guard Cavalry, with their standards, and the Infantry of the Guard.

THE IMPERIAL GENERAL STAFF. *Marshal Ney, the Emperor, and an aide-de-camp. Flat plastic figures, decorated on both sides. After original models by Leliepvre. (Mathiot Collection, Chantilly.)*

FIGURINES IN COLLECTIONS
AND MUSEUMS

In imitation of Asmodée, the demon in *Le Diable Boiteux*, let us lift up a rooftop, hither and yon, for a glance at figurine collectors throughout the world and a glimpse of their secrets.

In Germany, despite the large number of active enthusiasts, there will be few surprises. We have already had occasion to follow, on the far side of the Rhine, the birth of the modest tin soldier and his evolution to the status of a collector's item. The Germans have remained unswervingly faithful to the flat figurine, the *Zinnfigur*. Their occasional concern with *rondebosse* pieces was solely confined to toys, which, for the most part, were made for export.

As has been noted, they did look with favor on dioramas, which seem to have been the ultimate objective of most collectors. Many of them took pride in doing a large part of their own painting, and in building stage sets in which skill and ingenuity were displayed.

What were their favorite themes? Unquestionably, they were those suggested by ancient engravings and by significant episodes in their history.

But the tremendously wide range of choice offered by the major figurine makers—Heinrichssen, Ochel, and Neckel—when supplemented by the output of ever active amateurs, covered all of world history from the prehistoric era with its antediluvian animals down to modern times. Among the tens of thousands of different pieces, the most particular collector could make a satisfactory choice.

In addition to typically military topics—which obviously had the widest distribution but in which, for once, the wars of the First Empire did not have the dominant position—great popularity was accorded to ancient history, particularly that of Egypt and Rome. Next in order came the Middle Ages, then the Renaissance.

The reconstructions of regional or local history are of great interest because of their settings and because of the folk costumes. We have already

considered the dioramas of "Old Hamburg," by MM. Onken, K. Pless, Baumgart, and Bauthin, as well as the famous exhibits by M. Schmidt of Lado-Kiel.

Scenes from lyric drama also lend themselves to beautiful presentations, which some artist-collectors produce as accurate scale models.

The oldest of all clubs, the KLIO, provides the common ground upon which German collectors stand together. Its publications, *Die Zinnfigur* and the *Feldgrau*—in which recent developments are announced—have a very large circulation, even in foreign lands. Finally, friendly groups of collectors, often without official stand-

A SERGEANT OF THE KNOX ARTILLERY. *Revolutionary War. Behind the figurine, the flag of the Philadelphia City Troop. Figurine and flag by Colonel Stoddard. (Fort Sill Museum.)*

Above, left: ONE HUNDRED SEVENTH CAVALRY; OHIO NATIONAL GUARD, *1929;* right: FIRST OHIO VOLUNTEER CAVALRY, *1898*. Below, left: ONE HUNDRED SEVENTH CAVALRY, OHIO NATIONAL GUARD, *1935;* right: MAJOR OF THE FIRST SQUADRON, OHIO CAVALRY, *1916. By Berdou, Paris (Thoburn Collection, Cleveland.)*

ing, gather together in the larger towns for meetings at which information, and figurines, are exchanged.

In Austria, as in Germany, the majority of collectors concentrated on the flat tin figurine. For the average amateur, *ronde-bosse* subjects, as favored throughout Europe and in America, were too expensive. A single exception was found in the lead soldiers known, from the name of their producer, as *Wollnerfigüren*. In various scales, Wollner turned out troops of the former Austrian Army, and of the armies of several other countries. For use with them, appropriate accessories were also available.

Two well known Austrian collectors are now missing from the roll call: Krunert, the celebrated engraver, and Wilké, the military painter.

The latter also made numerous tin figures of which the best known, and the most eagerly sought, are his personages of the Thirty Years War.

Today the shops of Krunert, Scheibert, Parsen and Teuber have closed their doors. The one remaining commercial producer is Kober, of Vienna.

But Austrian collectors derive great benefit from a vigorous and very active club, The Society of 1683. Through the medium of a monthly Bulletin, members of that society are informed of purchase, sale and exchange offers, and at the same time they are apprised of the activities of collectors in other countries. They do, of course, suffer the handicap of a political isolation that places a limit upon contact with their colleagues in Western Europe.

Recognition should here be given to the distinctive creations of Helmut Krauhs, from whose hands we have manikins, about 30 mm. high, with head and hands carved from wood. They are dressed, armed and equipped by their maker, who thus reveals himself as an accomplished armorer.

His subjects are custom-made, for museums, and for an occasional amateur. Among them may be cited a series of fifty models of Austrian troops which, as exhibited in the Vienna Museum of Military History, cover the period from 1648 to 1848. His, also, are the several personnages of the time of Charles VI that are on display at the Regional Museum in the same city.

Austrian collectors, as has been intimated, have a fondness for the diorama, and are particularly interested in scale models that require the reproduction of fortifications, and of military vehicles of every kind and age. In such exhibits, 20 mm. figurines are generally employed. The most popular topics are the Thirty Years War, the Seven Years War, the Campaigns of Napoleon, and the Franco-German War of 1870.

Swiss collectors, like their German colleagues, confine their interest to flat tin figurines, almost to the exclusion of *ronde-bosse* figurines. Manufacturers of former days—like Aarau, whose castings may be seen in the National Swiss Museum at Zurich, and like the founder Hoffmann, have now disappeared. Amateur manufacturers, on the other hand, are most active. Their energies are devoted to enlarging their collections by the acquisition of novelties, which they are not unwilling to share with their friends. Among them the best known is Eugen Blum, of Zurich, who in addition to making figurines for his own collection, has continued some of the models made by his former friend Otto Gottstein of Leipzig, who died in London in 1952. His entourage includes Dr. J. Welti, Dr. Kurt Kollbrunner, Rudolf Hanhart and Max Weilemann, all of whom are devoting their best efforts to furthering the endeavours in which their honorary president was engaged for so many years.

The club of Swiss amateurs, *Figurina Helvetica*, was founded in 1939. Its first president was the late Monsieur Eugen Blum, who with great competence and skill directed and inspired that group. Unlike other associations of similar purpose, that club has elected to remain a closed organization that deliberately refrains from enlarging the circle of membership. As a group that is basically Swiss, the club admits as foreign corresponding members only a single collector from each country, and he must be a nonresident of his own land. The majority of its members look with disfavor upon conventions or expositions: in their view, a personal collection is a private affair, and as such is not a matter of concern to the general public.

That attitude seems unfortunate when one remembers the many superb groups of figurines created by Blum, including "The Battle of Morat," at which Charles the Bold was defeated by the Swiss, and the "Spanish Conquests in America," and the extraordinary "Elephants of Alexander and of Hannibal," which, as a matter of fact, were publicly exhibited in Paris in 1955.

Unexpectedly, considering Italy's admirable artistic past, Italian figurines seem to be several decades in arrears of the prevailing French techniques. There are eighteenth century tin subjects in the museum at Turin and some seventeenth century pieces in Milan, but we have no definite information as to their origin. Furthermore, about the only devotees of tin soldiers are collectors who use them in dioramas, and who are content with importations from other countries. There would appear to be no indigenous engravers or producers.

Collections in Italy are made up, for the most part, of *ronde-bosse* or *demi-ronde-bosse* figurines,

MARKET AT TENOCHTITLAN. *Pre-Columbian civilization, circa 1500. By Lacomblez. (Deconinck Collection, Brussels.)*

and of them the best are brought in either from Great Britain or France. Italian production is almost entirely limited to the Antononi establishment in Rome, and the output of that firm consists largely of toys from simple molds, with painting of uneven quality. In some instances however, as we have ascertained by experiment, their appearance can be greatly improved by careful painting after the rough edges have been trimmed away.

Much more interest, on the other hand, can be expressed in Italian editions of cardboard soldiers and in sheets of soldier pictures after the manner of Strasbourg or, better still, Epinal. In the Naples museum there is a very good collection of paper soldiers, published by Boldetti of Milan or by Ventura and Castiglione.

CHANGING THE GUARD. *At Hamburg, on the Gänsemarkt, in 1820. Flat figurines from various sources. Diorama by Baumgart, of Hamburg.*

That method of presentation, although considered obsolete by some people, appeals to many Italians, who with their own hands draw, cut out, and paint soldiers that bear witness to serious preliminary study of the history of uniforms. Among them should be mentioned Captain Gasparinetti, secretary general of the National Association of Italian Collectors, a group comprising some three hundred members, with headquarters in Rome. Much credit is due them for their concern with documentation and iconography, and also for their publication of pictures of uniforms covering the long period from 1660 to 1960.

It was an Italian political refugee, Ortelli, who in 1830 introduced the figurine into Spain. He made slate molds for his figurines, which were then cast in tin. Varying in height from 6 to 15 cm., his castings represented Spanish soldiers in the uniforms of that time. Some thirty years later he produced combatants of the African War of 1859/60, together with models of cannon. Then he turned to civil and religious subjects—dancers, bullfighters, horse-

drawn vehicles of all kinds, saints, and religious processions—in short, the past history of Barcelona. His molds, which are of some interest to specialists, may be seen at the Barcelona Museum of Popular Art. The painting of the subjects just described leaves something to be desired: it is more closely related to imagination than to fact.

Towards 1900, Casanellas and José Capelle undertook the manufacture of figurines representing all the armies of Europe. Joining forces with Millet, they established the Euloge Gonzalès Company, which supplied the markets of Spain and South America.

In 1929, Don Teodore Rodriguez arranged for the production in Germany of molds of all the dress uniforms then worn in the Spanish army. The resulting figurines were identified by the trademark "TEO." They are now eagerly sought because all the TEO equipment, like that of the Palomeque Company (well and widely known for its specialization in ancient

Above: left and right: GERMAN MARINES; center: AN ASKARI *(Native East African soldier). Circa 1910.* Below, left and right: OFFICERS OF THE IMPERIAL GERMAN NAVY; center: AN OFFICER OF THE MARINES. *Cardboard soldiers, designed and painted by Koekkoek for use in dioramas. (Military Museum, Leyden.)* ▶

◄ HUSSAR ON HORSEBACK. *Polychrome wood carving by Clémence. 1780. (Figurine Museum, Compiègne.)*

history) was destroyed during the civil war of 1936—39.

Worthy of mention because of their unusualness are the miniatures now being made by Alymer in Valencia. Their scale, 1:86, gives them a height of about 20 mm. Their execution, in-the-round, is pleasing.

Spanish collectors, generally speaking, appear to be much more interested in marshaling large numbers of effectives to form companies, battalions, and even complete regiments, than in the quality of the pieces employed. Don Arturo Llovera was awarded the Military Medal of Merit (non-combatant grade) for his scrupulous reproduction of an entire division. Nothing is lacking from that exhibit, which includes artillery, horse-drawn and automotive truck trains, and the full complement of 20,000 men, whose height is 54 mm. In a march past at regulation intervals the regimental column extends for three hundred yards!

Partisans of paper soldiers may also be found on the Iberian Peninsula. A collector in Madrid is said to have one hundred thousand of them, grouped in military formations.

A new association, the "Agrupación de Miniaturistas Militares," started at Barcelona in 1959, takes part in all the international expositions organized by similar but older groups in Europe. Its quarterly bulletin is well written, and unquestionably serves as an excellent source of documentation and inspiration.

For many years, England was content to import from Germany figurines intended for the amusement of children, without thought of local production. Public opinion, as we know, did not look with favor on the sale of games calculated to encourage militarism. The first step in that direction was taken, during the closing years of the nineteenth century, by William Britain. There was likewise Captain Siborne, whose dioramas on the Battle of Waterloo have been described. (Even today we do not know whence he obtained the vast number of figurines employed in that project.)

A SKIRMISH DURING THE CIVIL WAR. *Part of a group of ronde-bosse figures by Leliepvre. (Mathiot Collection, Chantilly.)*

The Army Museum, in Paris. Part of one of the "Ney" exhibition rooms in which groups and collections of figurines are on display.

Britain was the first to turn out figurines as hollow castings, a procedure that reduced both the weight of the pieces and the quantity of metal needed for the casting. It is interesting to note that his first and best customer proved to be Germany—a maker who became a buyer. Outstanding among his successes were "The Highlanders" and "The Life Guards," for both of which the horses are without the unesthetic, and now unnecessary base.

During the years between the two wars, Britain's firm became a leader in the international market, a fact due not only to very attractive prices, but to most careful execution, with painting that I consider superior to the "Lucotte" products of the same time.

Britain gave heed, of course, to the particular preferences of foreign customers. For each country a wide range of authentic uniforms was offered. It is still true that, from Madrid to Rome and Paris to Berlin, his "Soldiers and Troopers of the Scotch Guard" are highly prized. In fact, I know some French collectors who are so proud of having kept their "old Britains" that they have more than once repainted those figurines as a labor of love.

Such conspicuous success inevitably attracted imitators and—let us not mince words—junk makers who, in their eagerness to cash in on a good thing, descended to outright plagiarism without concern for the quality of the copies. No other maker of figurines was ever the victim of such scandalous purloining. John Garratt, in his remarkable book *Model Soldiers*, devotes interesting pages to such "specialists," of all nationalities. (They are found even in Japan). He accurately classifies them as pirates.

In 1955 the merger of Britain with Zang led to a trade name, "Herald Miniatures," that is well known to collectors.

In England as on the continent, the so-called lead soldier has become a collector's item. Hence, even though customers are not lacking in the toy market, makers of figurines are not slow to realize that there is a new outlet for their wares.

On the eve of World War II, Richard Courtenay produced his "Knights and Warriors of the Middle Ages." Strangely, his well-deserved reputation in that genre was more widespread on the far side of the Atlantic than on the continent, where his name was better known than his works. His characteristic technique is reflected in his personal attention to the finishing of figurines molded in quantity and of individual models.

The same genre, or at least the same theme, was exploited with equal success by Greenwood and by Miss Ball with figurines of many sizes, including 12, 20, 28, 54, and even 60 cm. They constituted ideal characters for the peopling of dioramas. We have already mentioned their use in the diorama "Debarkation in Normandy", as displayed in the Royal United Service Museum in London.

At the present time, one important British manufacturer is enjoying well-deserved success.

The Norman Newton Ltd. manufactures figurines designed by Charles Stadden, who has specialized in the armies of the Napoleonic

THE ROYAL ITALIAN NAVY. *Demi-ronde-bosse. Height 45 mm. Of Italian manufacture, circa 1920.*

Wars. Most popular was his series of *ronde-bosse* miniatures in the 25-mm. size. They are easily identified, not only by the thin metal bases to which they are soldered, but by expert engraving and very careful painting. Those miniatures, frequently employed by Stokes in his dioramas, are now exceedingly difficult to find.

Newton was one of the first figurine makers to make unpainted figurines available to collectors, thus enabling potential artists to achieve the long-cherished ambition of painting their own pieces. The products of the Newton firm were mounted with care. The purchaser could make his choice from soldiers in a variety of attitudes, and he did not look in vain for appropriate accessories of good quality.

Russell Gamage (whose output is distributed under the trade name "Rose Models") also offered the majority of his figurines in unpainted form. At the time of the coronation of Queen Elizabeth II he turned out a special group, limited to one thousand sets, which brought together the leading participants in that ceremony, from the Archbishop of Canterbury to the Yoemen of the Guard, pages, and heralds.

His "Horsemen of the Indian Army" are much admired for their typical silhouettes and for the quality of the painting. Quite recently he supplemented his Napoleonic War series with horse-drawn pieces of French and English artillery—to the delight of collectors whose collections are too often weak in *matériel* of that category.

The position achieved by English makers of *ronde-bosse* is enviable. By their initiative and sustained efforts they seem well qualified to meet the needs of an international clientele

A DRAGOON OF THE ITALIAN GUARDS. *Ronde-bosse figurine. Height 55 mm. (Marino Collection, Rome.)*

that has shown great interest in their new models. By the same token, they bid fair to take the lead in the European market.

In Great Britain, a land of traditions, there are many collectors. After a long period of dependence on the continent, they can now find at home a most abundant choice, and one that tends to encourage new vocations.

So general is the appeal of *ronde-bosse* figurines that the collectors of tin figurines now comprise a very small minority. The current production, of good quality and reasonably priced, is available to a large and growing public, which, as we have seen, is intrigued by the possibility of participating, actively and personally, in the setting up of collections.

What are the most popular themes and epochs? Unquestionably, the epic story of Napoleon. For the average Englishman it is a veritable cult, which, in its irresistible appeal, surpasses even Waterloo; in London as in Paris, the beginner's first purchase is a grenadier of the guard. Also popular are the Second Empire; the Crimean War and the allied combatants, including France; the colorful armies of the English colonies; the Middle Ages with the associated armor and armorial bearings; the Renaissance, with Henry VIII and Francis I. Finally, tradition dictates inclusion of the troops with which British collectors have fought, in various wars.

Among the museums in which dioramas are on exhibit, we have already mentioned those

CHINESE HORSEMAN. *Contemporaneous. Horse and rider of polychrome terra cotta, over a framework of iron wire. Height, 50 mm. (Sarramon Collection, Toulouse.)*

SHIP MODEL. *Demi-ronde-bosse. Of Italian manufacture, circa 1910.*

of London and Edinburg. In Windsor Castle there is a magnificent collection of figurines by Britain, and at York there are some unusual cardboard soldiers. And there is scarcely a regimental trophy room or an officer's club without a small museum in which, side by side with treasured war relics, there are representations of uniforms and reconstructions of military engagements of personal significance to the older members.

The British Model Soldiers Society, founded in London in 1935, publishes a bulletin that is devoted to documentation and recent developments. Some of the scholarly members of that society have taken the initiative in publishing color plates of soldiers' uniforms. English collectors, like their French colleagues, have an enthusiastic interest in the history of military costumes. For many of them, the collection is the ultimate reward of research as well as a decorative element in the home.

In Sweden, one name leads all the rest— Eriksson. His splendid *ronde-bosse* figurines, and particularly his eighteenth century horsemen, which are only 40 mm. high, are viewed with amazement by connoisseurs as well as by the unitiated. His peculiar technique involves the use of flexible molds and the building up of volume by successive, faceted layers which, when painted, give emphasis to the musculature and to the movement thereby suggested. The end product is one of the most remarkable creations that an enthusiast is likely to see.

It is through the courtesy of my friend and colleague Raymond Boverat (a collector-manufacturer of tin figurines) that I am enabled to include specific reference to some Swedish collectors. Among others he cites Berglund, of Stockholm, and his collection consecrated to the Thirty Years' War. For it Berglund produced a series of 28 mm. figurines that are admirably suited for the dioramas in which he successfully specializes.

Professor Rossner, after a residence of some years in Sweden, has become known for the period figurines he has cast in tin. They are for the most part civilian subjects, inspired by famous paintings or engravings of the seven-

teenth and eighteenth centuries, and executed in various sizes.

In conclusion, it may be noted that the majority of Swedish collectors prefer flat figurines, which generally speaking are of German origin.

Between Belgium and France there are the ties of a common language and shared military experiences. As might be expected, both have had an influence on Belgian figurines and on the tastes of Belgian collectors.

From the beginning, the tin figurine found simultaneous favor in Brussels and in Paris. (The collection virus strikes in the capital cities before spreading to the provinces. That is the law!) But in Belgium, the vogue of the flat soldier was of longer duration among people who were considered serious collectors. Their tardy interest in *ronde-bosse* figurines is un-

GROUP OF CHINESE HORSEMEN. *Obviously toys. Construction is reminiscent of the earliest of figurines. (Sarramon Collection, Toulouse.)*

derstandable, because there was no local production. From Germany, and then from France and Sweden, the Belgians imported tin soldiers, whose evolution toward the status of collectors' items they followed with keen interest. They also imported lead soldiers—of the toy category that had no great appeal—from France and Great Britain.

Simultaneously, however, with the initial appearance of figurines expressly made for collectors, a mounting wave of preference for *ronde-bosse* subjects was felt in Paris and London.

Just before World War II, a Belgian manufacturer named Steinbach started production of three-dimensional figurines of a larger than usual size. His admirable series "French Troops of the First Empire" (at which time, it will be remembered, Belgium was a part of France) included musicians of the period, horsemen having a height of some 80 mm., and many other personages, all of which were expertly painted. Those figurines, turned out over a ten-year span, were as popular in France as in Belgium.

The close relationship between the two countries led, naturally enough, to a quickening of interest in single models on the part of specialists in Belgium. There close attention was paid to foreign expositions, which are always a fruitful source of information and inspiration. Emulation brought into prominence a number of specialists who were highly skilled in the creation of exhibits. One of them, M. Lacomblez, quickly gained renown with the Aztec models that were presented at the 1961 Paris Exposition by Monsieur Deconick. A laudatory description of that work is made unnecessary by the illustrations of the two Aztec groups that are included in these pages. Of equal technical excellence, from the studio of the same artist, are the single models of the Burgundian period—a very popular subject in Belgium.

In 1938, Belgian amateurs organized The Belgian Society of Figurine Collectors, whose roster of honorary members includes some of the most famous names in the world of art and literature. Belgium, like Great Britain and France, is a land that pays high respect to civilian and military traditions. There honor is rightly given to Louis Leconte, the first curator of the Army Museum, to whose creation and development his entire lifetime was consecrated.

His erudition is recognized throughout all of Europe.

Belgian collectors, as a matter of fact, have been ardent in their researches on military history and the history of costumes. The study of those topics has become an indispensable adjunct of their avocation. Their society publishes a quarterly review: *La Figurine*, under the able editorship of its president, General Deleuze. That periodical, drawing its first inspiration from *Giberne* and *Passepoil* as formerly issued in France, quickly acquired an individual personality that can be credited alike to experienced editing and to the sections devoted to such specialities as tin figurines, lead soldiers, and documentation on costumes and armament. Each department, generously illustrated, provides its readers with a wealth of detail for which one usually looks in vain in earlier specialized works. There are also annotated illustrations of uniforms. Finally, there is a Bibliographical Review that not only covers recent publications by Belgian specialists, but gives abstracts of articles that have appeared in the bulletins of collectors associations in all other countries.

The magnitude of that accomplishment is emphasized by the fact that Belgium with nine million inhabitants, has some two hundred societies of collectors, whereas France, with its population of forty-five million, has six hundred and fifty clubs.

What do they collect? The First Empire, obviously, because many Belgian families have kept souvenirs of the days when their menfolk were soldiers and officers in the armies of Napoleon. But they also give attention to the history of Belgium, from the earliest times. Eggen, of Verviers, has shown us a re-creation of "The Construction of the Roman Road through the Ardennes," and "The Vision of St. Hubert" (the national saint). Others, whose names cannot be itemized here, have concentrated on the long and colorful period of Burgundian domination, and on the colonial troops of Belgium and her allies.

Active participation by Belgian collectors in all of the European fairs and expositions is an earnest of their genuine interest in union between the peoples of the smaller countries in Europe. Not limited by nominal frontiers, the worth of

their work is recognized throughout the world of the figurine.

The first International Congress of Figurine Collectors, held in Amsterdam in 1956, brought together prominent collectors from clubs in Germany, England, Belgium, Finland, France, Italy, Sweden, Switzerland, the United States, and, of course, Holland. That event was the more remarkable because, while the Low Countries have an association whose members specialize in tin soldiers (which there, as in Germany, are the only types collected), there is no commercial production of figurines.

During that congress there was advanced the novel and rather interesting proposal that there should be an international definition of colors, with index numbers. I was privileged to examine the proposed index. The resolution, I fear, is destined for oblivion.

As has been said, the only figurine known to the Dutch collector is the tin one, which is readily obtainable in the market that we have more than once described. While the museum

THE ALLIED MAJOR STAFF AT YORKTOWN. *Rochambeau, Washington, Lafayette, and officers of the French general staff. In the background, Chesapeake Bay. By the author*

at Leyden, a few miles from Amsterdam, exhibits interesting dioramas peopled with tin soldiers, it will also be remembered as possessing the only known collection of Koekkoek's cardboard soldiers. Those soldiers, which I believe are here illustrated for the first time, were greatly admired by members of the Congress. In subject matter, they cover the entire course of human history.

The United States is the country in which more, and more unusual, articles are collected than in any other land. There as elsewhere, the figurine did not become really popular until after World War I. It was one of the few "importations" military men returning to their homeland carried in their baggage.

It is recounted that, in the interval between the two wars, some male movie stars accumulated thousands, and even tens of thousands, of lead soldiers.

Purchases were generally made in complete sets, as produced by Britain, Lucotte, C.B.G., and other manufacturers. Some collectors felt that retention of the original boxes added to the value of the showing. Others, rightly, found it much more interesting to set up a military review, or a march-past, in a well lighted showcase.

Came then the Second World War and, in turn, the Cold War that is still with us. Many of those who had fought in Europe experienced, after returning to their homes, the desire to revisit the country where they had lived and suffered, but to see that land as something other than a dreary panorama of camps, momentary halting-places and battlegrounds. Like tourists the world around, they observed ways of life that were new to them. As they strolled hither

BRITISH BARRACKS AT TRENTON. *Part of a scale model, with ronde-bosse figurines by Imrie. (Trenton Museum, Trenton, New Jersey.)*

and yon, they picked up unusual knickknacks and curios as valued souvenirs of their travels. In England, Germany, France, and Italy they bought little soldiers.

Men who were too young to have been in the expeditionary corps were stationed in Europe for many years, either in the army of occupation or at the widespread military bases. There was ample leisure time, devoted by some to study, by others to sundry distractions. By different paths they reached similar findings.

Over the years I have maintained relationships, sometimes direct, with American collectors, both the important and the humble. In the course of conversation and correspondence with them, an effort has been made to decide *who* are the serious collectors, in a country whose broad expanse, dwarfing that of our own, is seldom realized here.

They may be divided into three categories. First are those to whom the figurine is little more than an interesting knicknack or a decorative item.

Then there are the hobbyists, to whom the figurine is a means of relaxation, albeit not in the sense of *le violon d'Ingres!* [1] They acquire unpainted figurines for the very real pleasure of decorating them with their own hands. For that pastime they have need (at least they did in the beginning, for the problem as we shall see has now been resolved) of documentation that, without critical intent, may be described as elementary. But such collectors, who comprise the majority, can scarcely claim the title of military historians because their interest in details is strictly limited to the simple requirements of their decorative projects.

The third category consists of collectors for whom the figurine is the end product of research on the history of costumes. Even if they do not have access to serious iconographic documentation, they are well informed on military history and they pay careful attention to every detail of the uniforms and to the accuracy with which flags are reproduced.

Who are they?

[1] Jean Auguste Dominique Ingres (1780-1867) was a distinguished French painter whose "second art" was the violin. Hence *le violon d'Ingres*, sometimes incorrectly considered to be synonymous with "hobby," has come to mean an artistic avocation.

As in Europe, they belong to all classes of society. Some, of course, are or were professional soldiers. But their ranks also include doctors, engineers, lawyers, manufacturers, businessmen, and artists. Many have turned to the figurine after having specialized in arms (in the United States, the number of collectors of arms is legion) or in models of airplanes, tanks, and similar *matériel*. Others, however, gained their introduction through iconography—engravings, pictures of uniforms, and, as a natural consequence, bibliography.

Personally, I would add a fourth category, comparable to the most important of European collectors: the true amateur who wants something better than the figurines shown in the illustrated catalogs, whose wide distribution is due to the publications of various associations of collectors.

To those catalogs the collectors who receive them regularly pay alert attention and from them the choice is made with confidence. Illustrated descriptions make plain the possible modifications and combinations, including the various bearings that can be imparted to horses. Catalog numbers make it easy to prepare the order, for which there is a special blank with columns for entry of every detail of the specification. A price list shows, in accordance with the number of pieces desired, the cost of packing and transportation. There is provision, I assure you, for everything, including the size of the paintbrush to be used. The catalog lists brushes, paints, and even wood bases appropriate for a single figurine or a group.

The experienced collector has long since made his choice of subjects for a given army, or for one or more definite periods of history. He has already supplemented available documentation by appropriate research, and has evaluated the inconsistencies of different sources. He then seeks, in France, England, or Germany, as may be appropriate, an artist of high repute.

The artist, after studying the folder of information that has been transmitted to him, makes sketches or watercolors of the figurine viewed from various angles. The sketches then go to the artisan who is considered best qualified to fashion the horse. For the rider, resort may be had to another craftsman.

Nothing has been left to chance, or to the fantasy of an absentminded workman. What does it matter if several months, or even longer, are required? The serious amateur realizes that the taking of infinite pains is rewarded by quality of the highest order.

It is only in recent years that the production of properly so-called collectors' figurines has been undertaken in the United States. Nothing is to be gained by enumerating the several makers of toys whose products do not rise above mediocrity.

Collectors, of necessity, had recourse to dealers or agents who imported from England or France figurines of various kinds, ranging from the collector's item to the special model. Many buyers, eliminating the middleman, dealt directly with original sources. In that action they were assisted by clubs which had been formed in various states and which, because of their connections and exchanges with European clubs, were helpful and dependable sources of information. Among them may be mentioned the Southern California Military Figures Society, the Miniature Figure Collectors of America, in Philadelphia, and—youngest, but by no means the least active—the Military Historical Society of New York. Each of them publishes a journal or bulletin, and all of them organize annual meetings or expositions and generously extend their co-operation to local fairs and shows.

Special recognition must be given to the Company of Military Collectors and Historians, of Providence, Rhode Island. Its membership includes such prominent experts in military history as Colonel F. Todd, Mrs. J. N. Brown, Major West; military painters like McBarron; advanced collectors like Ashton McDonnel, Captain Tily, M. C. Larter, and a host of others. Its quarterly *Journal*, which has been issued since 1949, quickly attained first place among specialized publications in the field. Because of the validity of its articles and the quality of its illustrations that journal has become the most valuable source of information on the American army, and as such it is of interest to specialists throughout the world.

American collectors who concern themselves with the flat tin figurine—and they are few indeed—were for the most part attracted to that style during sojourns in Germany, whence they now obtain their supplies. The great majority confine their interest to *ronde-bosse* figurines, either as prototypes or as components of dioramas, which, as we have seen, are very popular in the New World. Some collectors have independently developed the procedure followed by experienced collectors in France. They modify and embellish commercial figurines from which the paint has been removed.

A few years ago, I had the pleasure of meeting Mr. William Imrie when he was traveling in Europe to familiarize himself with the techniques employed by his colleagues on the continent. Today he is president of Hellenic Miniatures, a firm whose output reflects in subject choice and sales methods a serious psychological study of the market. Mr. Imrie's technique is in the tradition of the finest European specialists. His products may be had painted or unpainted. The gamut of possible transformations is explained to the customer, who receives very explicit instructions for painting.

Clearly, an ever-lengthening list of customers is required to support quantity production of articles as varied as figurines. At the same time, the buyer's interest must not be dampened by the conclusion that a given subject is too common because too many copies have been made.

Like the rest of the world, America has been attracted by the Napoleonic Wars, which have been so effectively popularized by motion pictures, illustrated publications, and books without number. The lead is taken by hussars, unquestionably because of the color and variety of their uniforms. Next in popularity are two great events in the history of the United States, the Revolutionary War and the Civil War. Episodes of the latter struggle, often most effectively dramatized, comprise for Northerners and Southerners alike an inexhaustible source of inspiration.

This is not to say that European armies are neglected. The Imperial Germany army has its devotees. And from English sources one can obtain a very complete group of British armies, with Highlanders as a center of attraction.

This brief review of American collections cannot be brought to a close without mention of several enlightened amateurs who, as it happens, are well known in France. The roll call must include Mr. Harlé, President of the Philadelphia Society; his predecessor in that office, Ashton McDonnell, who is one of the "greats"; Lyle Thoburn, of Cleveland, who has

spent many years on a meticulous reconstruction of American cavalry; Mr. Fox, of Albany, who specializes in the discoverers of America and the founders of the Republic; Peter Blum, the dynamic president of the young New York Society, and his colleagues Imrie, Munn, Murray, and Becker—all of whom as ardent enthusiasts gain new converts for the figurine. From the roster, which is long indeed, we cannot omit Colonel K. Gillaspey, of Washington.

Closely related to figurines is the work of Colonel von Schriltz, who now resides in France. There he is completing, in the form of color plates, a very extensive study of the uniforms worn by colonial troops between 1880 and 1900. That work will provide priceless documentation for future collectors.

In Canada the fraternity of collectors is at least sufficiently large to support the Canadian Historical Miniature Figures Society, with headquarters in Vancouver.

With the exception of a few toy manufacturers, Canadians do not actively engage in the making of figurines for collectors. That is understandable. They have ready access to British and American sources. They likewise have recourse to specialists in France, particularly for material concerned with the *ancien régime*. And the close kinship of the French-Canadians to their European cousins need not be stressed.

Proof of that cordial relationship is given by an enterprise privately undertaken in Montreal. In 1955 the Historical Society of Lake St. Louis took over a small blockhouse on the summit of Saint Helena Island, where it set up a museum of arms, uniforms, and figurines that recapitulated Canadian history from 1492 to 1760. The additional space that soon proved necessary was made available through the co-operation of the Montreal Park Department, which authorized the use of part of the arsenal barracks that were built on that island after the War of 1812. The history of the nation is there unfurled by means of large-scale maps, increasingly complete iconography, and dioramas with *ronde-bosse* figurines, most of which were made in France. Those dioramas commemorate the more outstanding episodes of the "French Period."

Uniformed manikins, with collections of arms and other *matériel* of the same period, round out the exhibits in that museum, where it has been necessary every year to open new display rooms in the barracks and casemates.

We now approach the closing pages of this chapter in which we have taken a quick glance at the many lands where, for one reason or another, the figurine enjoys popularity. Examples have been cited for the sole purpose of setting forth the tastes and tendencies peculiar to each nation. We have deliberately omitted countries on which our personal information is not adequate.

With one or two other nations, France has played an active and at times a preponderent part in the evolution of the figurine. For that reason, I have mentioned, from chapter to chapter, the most prominent names (although there are certainly others of importance) of men who were, in their respective specialities, craftsmen of the highest rank. It should be said that each of them, at the beginning, was an amateur who labored without thought of present or future profit. If, as was natural, some subsequently commercialized their production,

that step was taken without prejudice to the collector's characteristic appreciation of a job well done.

Here, as elsewhere, collectors are found at all levels of society, with corresponding differences in their financial means. But they have one thing in common—the desire to increase their knowledge as they increase their collections, of which they recognize that a library, however modest, is an integral part. From a work of reference that is beyond their means, they take notes and make photographs, tracings, or even rough sketches of everything that is germane to their projects.

Each, at the outset, establishes for himself a goal that, though perhaps distant, is very definite. A renowned Parisian amateur devoted more than fifty years to the realization of a youthful dream—that of creating with figurines a veritable

One of the salons in Anderson House, Washington, D.C., the Museum of the Cincinnati. Between replicas of French flags that saw service during the Revolutionary War, there are showcases with groups of figurines clad in the various uniforms of Rochambeau's expeditionary corps.

GERMAN CHASSEUR *and* THOMPSON'S PENNSYLVANIA RIFLE-
MAN. *Period of the Revolutionary War. Ronde-bosse
figurines by Imrie. (Risley Collection, New York.)*

history of France, with its kings and famous
generals. Subsequently he added important
horsemen, in which he had become interested
as the work progressed. Many were the years
of research and labor that preceded the housing,
in his showcases, of the long-awaited guests.
Ultimately, the uninterrupted cavalcade successfully depicted the continuity of French
history, with its dark days and its episodes
of glory.

There is another figurine enthusiast of whom
it might be said that he was born a collector.
The impetus came from his father, who had
preserved childhood toys that, in his day, were
treated with respect. The resulting exhibit is
probably unique. The son proceded with greater
eclecticism. He selected the models that were
most truly representative of their several genres.
In his showcases one may follow the evolution
of the figurine through its successive meta-
morphoses, observing, the while, examples of
the most diverse methods of expression.

A forty-year accumulation of specimens chosen from the best of tin soldiers produced
throughout Europe, and painted by the most
accomplished of artists, poses a serious problem:
how can they be protected and arranged? The
galleries of a large museum would not enable
an exhibitor to do justice to all of them.

On entering this collector's vast library, one
is struck by the systematic arrangement of
books in beautiful bindings. There is only an
occasional showcase, with a small group of
figurines standing in diffused light. Folding doors
open to reveal shelves on which other volumes
of identical format are aligned in battle formation, and numbered. Each of those books is,
in reality, a glass-covered box containing a
valuable exhibit. A key is provided to the
whole by a card index that itemizes the creator,
the engraver, the painter, and even the date
of acquisition.

The owner is a dramatic artist whose talents
and affability are known and admired on both
sides of the Atlantic. As was appropriate for a
man of the theater, his collection was for years
an integral part of the décor. And what a décor!

It was reached by a special staircase, from which one stepped into the Emperor's striped canvas tent. Here and there were drums, a few weapons, and small showcases containing remarkable miniature models of headgear, helmets, armor, and even uniforms, which seemed to be waiting, on their supports, for someone to don them. Roundabout were framed showings, in exquisite tin miniatures, of the pomp of tournaments ... the magnificent Knights of the Golden Fleece, with heralds, pages, and ladies in the tapering headdresses of that time. Hidden projectors illuminated the exhibits, with an effect that was delightfully unreal. In his new residence the décor could not be duplicated, but the display cases, beloved and faithful companions of their master, are all in place.

Books, and still more books, everywhere— on the mantelpiece, in precarious piles on the floor, and on the large worktable, where they scarcely leave writing space for this indefatigable military historian, who interrupts his research only long enough to attend to the promotions of the officers of the General Staff.

But on the bookshelf that faces him, in front of the books that he most frequently consults, there is a mounted Napoleon in the best Lucotte style. From the gray riding coat some of the paint has peeled away. Well do I know the figurine. More than once have I patched up the horse when an unfortunate brushstroke had been equivalent to another Ratisbonne for the Emperor!

You ask whether the man is a collector? He is, indeed. His collection, probably the most elaborate in the world, is certainly the greatest in France.

In France, as you see, all the collectors are poets.

Having rashly introduced you to some of them, I again raise the traditional question: what do they collect? In the first instance, tin figurines, of which we shall speak first, in honor of their seniority.

Their popularity has remained surprisingly constant. To them more than one fourth of all collectors remain faithful. Many who collect them also make them. We have already mentioned C.-F. Keller, whose creations provided happy inspiration for Major Borie, of Orleans, in his study of the Empire; Raymond Bovaret, for reproducing the campaigns in Russia and Belgium, as well as for his hussars; the work of Jacques Laurent, Pierre Fouré, and O' Callaghan in Paris, to say nothing of Jacques Meyniel and the ingenuity with which he has constructed modern motorized and armored *matériel*.

They have, one and all, enlarged and enriched the lesser figurine groups that had been available in other countries. The greater credit is theirs because at the present time they alone in France are bringing out new pieces in tin. (The house of Mignot has produced little indeed since the last war.)

There is, in addition, a legion of enlightened enthusiasts who cannot be named without imparting to this volume directory characteristics that are beyond its scope. Even so, one cannot pass over in silence such names as Pierre Brétégnier and Armand Gritton. And it should be added that every public exposition affords the opportunity of meeting highly skilled painters and accomplished creators of dioramas.

While some of the more conservative collectors were not at first impressed by the rising popularity of *ronde-bosse* figurines, it was not long before they began to show interest in the new genre. As good sportsmen they were soon riding the two hobbies abreast.

C.-F. Keller was the first to set the example, by choosing *ronde-bosse* figurines for his "Retrospective View of the Flags of Swiss Regiments in the Service of France and other Countries."

Mme. Métayer added every year to her series of "Little Soldiers of France." She was accorded the honor, for such it is, of seeing her work plagiarized by foreign manufacturers under titles as varied as they were unfair. Thereby her reputation was enhanced rather than harmed.

Much later, toward 1954, Robert Dumesnil brought out his folk subjects of the Basque provinces and Auvergne. These were followed by "French Infantry under the Empire," and by his excellent "Marine Guards." He is now engaged in creating a complete "Military Band." Dumesnil leaves nothing to other hands. He makes his own models and his own production molds—truly an exceptional achievement, given the material and technical difficulties that must be surmounted to assure the quality that characterizes his work.

Fouillé, a marine artist whose many paintings have found a place in museums and private collections, has recently developed an entirely new genre—the statuette figurine. Using *ronde-bosse* technique, but on a much larger scale (8.4:100), he created an infantryman who, base included, stands 20 cm. high, and a horseman whose height is 26 cm. The resulting detail and the quality of the painting may be judged from the accompanying illustrations.

In addition to such manufacturers, and to the sources already mentioned for flat soldiers, our collectors may have recourse to men who specialize in the individual model, though their number is not large. Their ill-rewarded endeavor requires great perseverence and a high measure of modesty, in addition to an artistic ability that is here of greater importance than technique. Modesty is mentioned because, despite the relatively high price of the models, their quality imposes a low limit on production.

If the maker were tempted by any subterfuge that might result in economy of time (I cannot write economy of personnel), the sharp-eyed buyer would instantly discern the difference, and his hasty judgement would not be complimentary. In short, the situation is one in which time must be disregarded, because nothing counts but the result. Makers of individual models, enjoying the patronage of the more important French and foreign collectors, strive to deserve that honor as increasingly subtle techniques enable them to improve on their own best works. Right, M. Berdou? Right, Mlle Desfontaines? One might ask the same question of M. Zuber, a couturier whom no one has surpassed in one of the oldest of arts, that of feminine style.

We have introduced, not the individuals, but their works, so that our readers to whom they were unknown may have the pleasure of discovering their accomplishments.

On more than one occasion, reference has been made to Eugène Leliepvre who, however, stands somewhat apart from the men who have just been mentioned. For that military painter, the figurine *is a violon d'Ingres*, for which only limited time can be spared from his many assignments. That is why (exception made for these pages) his work can only be seen in the Mathiot Collection.

That collection, though one of the finest in France, is not well known because less than a year has elapsed since its transfer from Algeria to the mainland. Its showcases house only *ronde-bosse* figurines. It will, I believe, be many months before Leliepvre can properly display his thousands of tin figurines, not to mention what I consider to be the most comprehensive ensemble of military accouterments in miniature —weapons, shakos, caps, armor, saddlery, and trappings.

It is from his displays that we have, with his gracious permission, composed the cover of this volume. From the same source we have taken many illustrations, as for example "The Watering Trough," surrounded by light horse of 1786; "The Farrier" (after a canvas by Lenfant), with mounted grenadiers of 1745; a portion of "A Skirmish during the War of Secession," and many other beautiful creations.

Let me not forget the figurine enthusiasts themselves, of whom so many have essayed the unrewarding but thrilling art of "creation;" it matters not that so much effort meets with tardy reward. The creators still regard their "children" with prejudiced eyes. They know that practice makes perfect, that perseverance will one day be crowned with victory.

France shares with Germany the honor of having established a figurine museum, and one that is frequented by tourists because it is set up in the famous Compiègne Hôtel de Ville, in the immediate vicinity of the palace.

It was in 1948 that Armand Gritton, former president of the Society of Figurine Collectors, obtained municipal authority, not only for the use of that space, but for the display of a large collection of soldiers that had been willed to the city some twenty years earlier.

In addition to the extraordinary wood carvings by Clemence, whose work we have already seen, the museum possesses two masterpieces. The first, a diorama of the Battle of Waterloo, covers thirty-one square yards. Its twelve thousand tin figures reproduce the situation that existed between 4.00 and 5.00 p.m. on the day of the battle. The creator was M. Laurent, a fervent disciple of the First Empire, who is said to have devoted more than fifteen years to its execution.

Entirely different is the "Bétheny Review" which took place in 1901, in the presence of the Czar and President Loubet, at the Châlons Military Camp. Twelve thousand *demi-ronde-bosse* figurines represent the whole prewar French

army with red pantaloons, glittering cuirassiers, hussars and light cavalry.

Since its inception, the Compiègne Museum has been enriched by gifts from collectors and by sundry acquisitions, including numerous dioramas that benefit from their location in large, well lighted rooms. There are also retrospective views of archery throughout the ages, and artillery from its very beginning.

Appropriately, the curator is himself an experienced collector, as visitors are quick to realize when his guidance is sought.

The Army Museum at the Hôtel des Invalides —visited every day by tourists, from all over rhe world, who come to admire the most impressive mementos of our military glory— has consecrated three "Ney" rooms[1] to the

[1] I.e. display rooms named for Marshal Ney, an illustrious warrior in the days of the Revolution and the Empire.

One of the casemates of the old Montreal arsenal, on St. Helena Island, furnished by the Montreal Military Museum. In the showcases, groups of figurines reproduce important happenings of the French Period.

figurine. There we have already had a glimpse of that dean of dioramas, "The Battle of Dettingen."

The entire display consists essentially of three collections:

The Würtz Collection, previously mentioned, was willed to the museum in 1899. It comprises some twenty thousand Strasbourg soldiers, which are notable for very excellent painting.

The Bernard Franck Collection was acquired in 1935 by Jacques Violet, who gave it to the museum. Its complement of two hundred and forty small-scale figures (mostly foot soldiers having a height of about 40 cm.) recapitulates the history of French troops from the days of the Gauls down to and including the First

Empire. In spite of minor inaccuracies, unavoidable at the time when the figurines were made, the detail of the reconstruction is admirable. The headgear, body-armor, helmets and armament are perfect.

Finally the Ridder Collection given to the museum in 1946, is by far the most important, in size and interest.

On the walls there are glassed-in tableaux containing priceless old tin soldiers, by Allgeyer, for which one would look in vain today. The showcases are filled with small, skillfully executed dioramas peopled with some of the thirty or forty thousand subjects that Heinrichssen produced, in the 30-mm. size, on topics ranging from the dawn of history to the Third Republic.

But of greatest interest to enthusiasts are the cases that display large flat figurines of the same origin. The exhibits, truly impressive, cover "The Army of Frederick the Great and his Bodyguards" (standing 70, 75, and 77 mm.

high); the whole of Germany—Hanover, Bavaria, etc.; Austria, Great Britain, Denmark, Sweden, Belgium, Holland, Switzerland, Poland, Spain, Italy, the Vatican, Turkey, Russia, and the countries of North and South America.

Ronde-bosse techniques are represented by the splendid products of Britain and Lucotte, with particular emphasis on the artillery of all European countries. Since a description of such important exhibits is impossible, it is hoped that the foregoing references may encourage the reader to see them for himself, on the spot.

What is to be the future, in France of the figurine, considered in the broadest sense of that term and evaluated from the viewpoint of the many aspects that we have discussed? Assuredly, it will differ from the figurine that has evolved during the past thirty years. For only thirty years have elapsed since the first handful of amateurs decided to co-operate in efforts that had been individual and isolated.

JACQUES CARTIER AND AN INDIAN. *Ronde-bosse figurines by the author. (Military Museum, Montreal.)*

TRAPPER AND INDIAN, IN NORTHERN CANADA. *By the author. (Military Museum, Montreal.)*

Some of them may have attended the famous International Exposition at Leipzig, the last showing organized by the illustrious Otto Gott-stein before he took the lonely road to exile. If so, they brought back much useful infor-mation, as well as realization of what they might in turn achieve in an association seriously concerned with construction.

Success was granted to them, and to their followers. Their first exposition, modest indeed, was held in 1932 at the shop of Le Plat d'Etain. Their thirteenth show, at the Palais de Chaillot, has just closed its doors. For the first time, there was significant foreign participation. Germany, Belgium, Spain, and Great Britain were worthily represented.

This rapid, and therefore rather superficial, review will have served to give the reader some familiarity with the Figurine; some under-standing of the status which it has acquired,
throughout the world, during the past quarter-century.

Examples have been cited to emphasize the fact that amateurs in many lands have success-fully illustrated their history... local, regional, or national... with miniature personages who thus become the colorful symbols of that history.

What materials will hereafter be employed in the creation of such personages? It matters not. Any process, any medium of expression, is good ... if the end product reflects study and research of the sort that increases the knowledge and enriches the mind of the creator.

The continuing exchange of ideas between groups whose common purpose is expressed in different languages needs must contribute to a fuller understanding between peoples, hitherto alien each to the other, who are today united in one community of interest: the History of Mankind.

SELECTED BIBLIOGRAPHY

D'ALLEMAGNE, Henri-René: *Histoire des Jouets*, Paris 1903.
ARMONT, Paul: *Soldats d'hier et d'aujourd'hui*, Paris 1929.
BARD, Bob: *Making and Collecting Military Miniatures*, New York, 1957.
BERLING, Carl: *Altes Zinn*, Leipzig 1919.
BERNARD, Jean: *Le jouet français*, Paris 1926.
BOESCH, Hans: *Kinderleben in der deutschen Vergangenheit*, Leipzig 1900.
BONNES, August: *Die Zinngießerfamilie Meyerheine*, Potsdam 1937.
BUCQUOY, E. L. Cdt, *Bréviaire du Collectionneur*, Nancy 1953.
Bulletin de la Société des Collectionneurs de Figurines, Paris 1931-1961.
Catalogue de l'„Exposition de soldats artistiques", Paris 1929.
CLARETIE, Léo: *Les jouets historiques*, Paris 1894.
ELGSTRÖM, Ossian: *Wie man mit Zinnsoldaten Krieg führt*, Leipzig 1912.
FLOERICKE, Karl: *Strategie und Taktik des Spiels mit Bleisoldaten*, Dresden 1924.
FORGEAIS: *Notice sur les plombs trouvés dans la Seine*, Paris 1858.
GARRATT John G.: *Model Soldiers, a collectors guide*, London 1959.
GOTTSTEIN, Otto: *The King's armies through the ages — in Dioramas, The Royal United Services Museum*, London 1950.
HAMPE, Theodor: *Der Zinnsoldat, ein deutsches Spielzeug*, Berlin 1924.
HEINRICHSEN, Ernst: *Preis- und Warenverzeichnis*, Nürnberg 1900.
HELM, Robert: *Nürnberger Zinnfiguren*, Nürnberg 1935.
JACKSON, Mrs. N.: *Toys of Other Days*, London 1908.
KELLER, Charles-Félix: *Eloge des soldats fins*, Paris 1928.
MARSY, A. de: *Clémence et ses Soldats de Bois*, Compiègne 1858.
MARTIN, Paul: *Les Petits Soldats de Strasbourg*, Straßburg 1950.
MARTIN, Paul: *Der Standhafte Zinnsoldat*, Stuttgart 1961.
MARTIN, Paul et VAILLANT M.: *Le Monde merveilleux des soldats de plomb*, Paris 1959.
National Park Service: *The siege of Yorktown*, Washington 1957.
PAARDEKOOPER A. C.: *Notizen über die Soldaten von Koekkoek*, Leyden 1961.
PICARD, Marcel: *Soldats de Rêve*, Paris.
SCHIRMER, Friedrich: *Umgang mit Zinnfiguren*, Burgdorf-Han. 1957.
SENST, Otto: *Die Spielwarenindustrie von Fürth und Nürnberg*, Erlangen 1901.
TODD, F. Colonel: *Notizen über die Dioramen des West-Point Museums*, 1961.
TSCHISCHNITZ, Theodor von: *Anleitung zum Kriegsspiel*, Neisse 1862.
WELLS, H. G.: *Little Wars*, London 1913.
WHITE, George: *A Book of Toys*, 1946.

SOURCES OF ILLUSTRATIONS

Archives Photographiques: pages 4, 5.
Brunon: pages 18, 81.
Dunlop: page 121.
Fleming: pages 62, 63.
Giraudon: pages 3, 6.
Scott: page 31.
U.S. Army: page 60.

Most of the illustrations were taken by the photographer
Claude Michaelides, Paris.